Remember Me

How letters from my Civil War uncle helped me confront my childhood CIA attacker

BENJAMIN KENDRICK BUCKLEY

REMEMBER ME: HOW LETTERS FROM MY CIVIL WAR UNCLE HELPED ME CONFRONT MY CHILDHOOD CIA ATTACKER
COPYRIGHT © 2023/2024 BENJAMIN KENDRICK BUCKLEY

Published by:
Trine Day LLC
PO Box 577
Walterville, OR 97489
1-800-556-2012
www.TrineDay.com
TrineDay@icloud.com

Library of Congress Control Number: 2024941539

Buckley, Benjamin Kendrick.
–1st ed.
p. cm.

Epub (ISBN-13) 978-1-63424-474-9
Trade Paperback (ISBN-13) 978-1-63424-473-2
1. Civil War letters of Henry Christopher Binns Kendrick (1861-1863). 2. United States History Civil War, 1861-1865 Personal narratives. 3. United States. Central Intelligence Agency Corrupt practices. 4. Project MKULTRA (U.S.). 5. Sexual abuse victims United States. I. Buckley, Benjamin Kendrick. Title

FIRST EDITION
10 9 8 7 6 5 4 3 2 1

Credit cover art depicting H.C. to Michael Timothy Davis of Shepardstown West Virginia. Michael stylized the painting from the original Ambrotype of H.C. Taken in 1861 shown

Printed in the USA
Distribution to the Trade by:
Independent Publishers Group (IPG)
814 North Franklin Street
Chicago, Illinois 60610
312.337.0747
www.ipgbook.com

Publisher's Foreword

Oh we'll rally round the flag, boys, we'll rally once again,
Shouting the battle cry of freedom,
And we'll rally from the hillside, we'll gather from the plain,
Shouting the battle cry of freedom.
The Union forever, hurrah! boys, hurrah!
Down with the traitors, up with the stars;
While we rally round the flag, boys, we rally once again,
Shouting the battle cry of freedom!
— George Frederick Root, 1862

Our flag is proudly floating, On the land and on the main,
Shout, shout, the battle cry of Freedom;
Beneath it oft we've conquered, And will conquer oft again,
Shout, shout, the battle cry of Freedom.
Our Dixie forever, she's never at a loss
Down with the eagle and up with the cross
While we rally 'round the Bonnie flag, we'll rally once again,
Shout, shout the battle cry of Freedom!
— H. L. Schreiner and lyricist W. H. Barnes, 1863

War generally isn't a "fun" activity. Why does war happen? Do we learn from it? Do they advance the cause of humanity? What makes a good war? Are all wars bad? Coming of age in the 1950s and '60s, war was a constant. Frst there was our fathers and other relatives who had fought in WWII. They generally didn't talk much about it, but the culture sure did. We were the good guys, along our allies; Germany, Italy and Japan were the bad guys in countless movies and television shows. We always won, and were morally correct.

Then came the Vietnam "police action," as the undeclared war was called in its early days. I remember a day around 1965 when after watching the nightly news with my family, my father turned to me and asked what I thought about the conflict. I gave him a flip teenage answer. I said, "Well, you have a sack of hand grenades, throw them in the rice paddies and win it for the good guys wearing the white hats." *My Dad said we had to have a talk.*

I had forgot all about that conversation until in 1969 on the day before my twentieth birthday, Dad said,"It's time for that talk." I had forgotten all about it. I had dropped college, got married, had a six-month-old daughter, started a record store and was producing rock and roll shows. *I was having a good time.*

Dad had a professor friend, Dr. D.F. Fleming visiting, and they led me into a room and sat me down. Dad said, "The Vietnam War is about Drugs. There are the secret societies behind it. Communism is all a sham, these same secret societies are behind it. It is all a big game?" He lost me. I was befuddled. Then they told me all, about my Dad's almost 20-years in US intelligence services. It took me years to understand, but the conversation started my journey into a subject I call CIA-Drugs.

Benjamin Buckley began his journey a bit differently. He adroitly tells his tale in *Remember Me: How Letters From My Civil War Uncle Helped Me Confront My Childhood CIA Attacker* by writing to his great Uncle Henry Christopher Binns Kendrick during his time as a young soldier in the Civil War. TrineDay is honored to publish this perceptive, poignant and sometimes heart-breaking tale – one that could only be written ... today.

> *War, huh, yeah*
> *What is it good for?*
> *Absolutely nothing, uhh*
> *– Barrett Strong & Norman Whitfield*

Onward to the Utmost of Futures!
Peace,
RA "Kris" Millegan
Publisher
TrineDay
July 16, 2024

Dedicated to those who created the UDHR, those who signed it, and those who believe and abide.

CONTENTS

PREFACE

From 1960 to 1963 I attended Nellie Custis Elementary School in Arlington, Virginia. During those years, the United States of America was in the midst of celebrating the Civil War centennial, and simultaneously, embroiled in the Cold War with the Union of Soviet Socialist Republics. Both events were a part of the times, and Arlington, Virginia was in many ways the center stage for both the Civil War and the Cold War.

My little school was less than two miles from the Pentagon and less than five miles to Robert E. Lee's home. As a boy, I had been to Lee's home and the Pentagon many times. Many Civil War battles were fought near my home, perhaps within less than 200 miles. If the Cold War became hot, perhaps the first target would've been the Pentagon.

However, as a young boy, my thoughts quickly left the Cold War problems in favor of playing ball games, the Ringling Brothers Circus, trains, planes, boats, and making friends. At the end of the school day some of the students, including myself, would walk across 23rd Street to the Potomac Market to purchase candy or drinks. Amongst the displays of candy were five cent packs of Civil War News Cards. On the front of the cards was a colorful, and sometimes gory, scene of a Civil War battle or event, on the back was the news article describing the scene that was on the front of the card. The art captivated my imagination. The cards served The Topps Company, Inc., I am sure, very well; and was a home run outside the baseball diamond!

One of my teachers at Nellie Custis School brought her grandmother into class one day. She was over 100 years old, and I was quite astonished because she was born before the Civil War! I felt close to the war only because I knew her, and she had lived through it as a young lady.

Not until I grew older did I realize the tragedy of the war. Or at least I thought so. I don't understand and can't even grasp the reasoning, even today, for a blood sacrifice.

In 2020, while researching on the internet to learn more about the writings of my grandfather, Benjamin Burks Kendrick (1884-1946), who was a professor of history at the Women's College of the University of North Carolina. I was surprised to discover a set of letters written to his family back home in Georgia by his uncle, Henry Christopher Binns Kendrick, my great-grand uncle, from the front lines of the U.S. Civil War.

It appears my grandfather donated the letters to the University of North Carolina during his term as professor at the University. Henry Christopher Binns Kendrick, H. C. Kendrick, as he was known, was an uncle to my grandfather. My grandfather had six uncles, all of whom served as Confederate Civil War Soldiers from Talbot County, Georgia.

Talbot County was founded in 1827. This is where the Benjamin Burks Kendrick (BBK) Family Plantation was located. My great-great-grandfather BBK arrived in Talbot County in 1829. The population nearly tripled between 1830 and 1840. Today the population may be less than it was in 1830. From most accounts the area was in an economic boom prior to the Civil War. More than half the population was in bondage. The Kendrick household owned slaves, and also, rented slaves as needed. Benjamin and his wife, Frances Lloyd, had nine children and education was held in high regard. At the funeral of Benjamin Burks Kendrick, in 1873, one of his friends who had known him as Burks since his first coming to Talbot County said of him,

> I am not saying this in idle praise or eulogy, but from the first to last Burks Kendrick has been the most useful man in our county. There have been others who had more wealth, others who had more education, but none who had a better kinder heart and proved it by his daily life and contact with his fellow men. "Love thy neighbor as thyself" was carried out in word and deed.

Perhaps the kind words expressed by a close friend can give you a glimpse into the home of H.C. Kendrick.

H.C. Kendrick (H.C. or Chris) was the 6th child of Benjamin Burks and Frances Lloyd Kendrick. He was born in December 1840. He was only 20 years old when he enlisted in the Talbot Guards, Company E, Regiment 9, Georgia Volunteer Infantry. H.C. rose to the rank of first sergeant and was a bridge between the enlisted and commissioned soldiers. A niece of H.C., Leila Burks Kendrick, noted in her Biography of Benjamin Burks Kendrick (BBK 1807-1873) that *"Chris, the studious thoughtful lad who gave such promise of becoming a great man"* was the second son to go to war, John was the first.

The letters herein were written by Henry Christopher Binns Kendrick. He was one of six uncles of my grandfather. My grandfather's father (William Thomas Kendrick 1843-1921) and six uncles made a total of seven men (5 brothers and 2 brothers-in-law) from the Kendrick Family of Talbot County, Georgia, immersing themselves into a cruel Civil War that nearly put an end to our young republic.

After finding these letters, I felt compelled to share them with you.

Both of the stories in this book needed to be told. Primarily from a selfish standpoint. The Civil War letters, in particular, compelled me to re-examine my childhood fascination with the Civil War.

Although the letters are old, I thought the letters were important and pertinent today as when they were written. Words, spellings, and punctuation within the letters have been left exactly how H.C. had written them. Some portions have been clarified by deducing the missing words when the script or letter was damaged. So, I have done my best to show the letters as they were written.

Today our country seems divided - red and blue. And as the sayings go, from many years past....

> *Those who cannot remember the past are condemned to repeat it.*
> – George Santayana, *The Life of Reason*, 1905.

And...

> *Only the dead have seen the end of war.*
> – George Santayana, *Soliloquies in England*, 1924.

The depredation and lost lives of both sides have had a profound impact that has not, or may never be reconciled. The families that were affected will never be made whole again. The collection of letters here in this book were written by my great-grand uncle, you will come to know him as H.C. or Chris. His words speak from the grave, and his fate was like so many other young men of his generation.

There was a young lady named Levicie Maddox who H.C. was engaged. His fate as you will discover lead her to marry another member of the Kendrick Family, and thereby she became my Great-Grandmother. Perhaps my own life is owed to H.C. and his last day of life at a wheatfield in Pennsylvania.

It was strange to know how most of the soldiers chose which side they would fight on simply by birth. I am certain if H.C. was from Massachusetts which is where the Kendrick Family arrived in the 1600s he would've enlisted in the Northern Cause.

This leaves me with the notion that his decision to join the Confederacy was not his own.

So, I assume he was influenced by a power that overruled his own critical thinking skills. If this is true, who was the influencer? The leadership of our country enlisted these young people into a conflict that convinced them to sacrifice their own lives, willingly.

Should 'We the People' question our leadership when asked to make the ultimate sacrifice, or should we simply submit? My hope is, that consent for a blood sacrifice will be avoided whenever possible for the progress of man. Entries to war ledgers are exclusively red- red blood and red ink.

Each of these letters is answered by me. Everyone has a story and I love sharing stories. I wanted to share parts of my life with the spirit I met that fateful Autumn Day. When I first read his letters, I heard him mention the phrase, 'Remember Me.' The words suddenly captured my sober attention, sadly, because he was nearly forgotten.

Perhaps by sharing his letters his spirit might rejoice. And rest his soul in peace.

I am once again thrust into study of the Civil War. Today though, I have experience gained from maturity, at least I think so. With the help of LTC Henry Persons Jr. (US ARMY-RET.), and my lovely partner, Roberta Meade, I was able to transcribe the letters contained in this book. Paul Guzzo helped me to organize the thoughts into the framework of a book. My good friend Antony Becker, my cousin Bonnie E. Kendrick, and many others helped edit, provide family histories, and pertinent facts. Thanks to John Malone who walked Gettysburg Battlefield Park with Roberta and me during the COVID pandemic. I am truly grateful to all of the relatives and friends who have helped.

May the words of Christopher Kendrick shine light on one of the darkest times of the American Experience.

BKB.

The Letters

LETTER 1

Atlanta, Ga.

June 15th, 1861

Dear father,

We are now in the actual service. We are ordered to Richmond, Virginia. We will start tomorrow evening to realize the realities of contention.

Father we get plenty to eat, good enough too. The new confederate government is a good friend of ours she gives us plenty to eat, to ware, and to do. You know that that is that for which I am willing to rush into all most anything that is creditable. We consider this so.

Father, we have elected Captain Goulding Colonel of the regiment with whom the regiment is pleased. I am well pleased my-self and two [of] the cleverest men for our lieutenant colonel and major that you ever saw in your life. I would write to you who will be our Captain, but I have not the time.

One of the men from Geneva is going to start home directly by whom I intend to send this letter and also my ambrotype to Geneva. The latter will be attended by my love for you all.

The time is near at hand in which we will drill consequently I cannot write much more. The drum is beating for drill now. I am well and have been ever since I left home.

I am writing on a trunk, and you cannot expect much, st time.

All receive my love.
H.C. Kendrick.

LETTER 1 REPLY

Dear H.C.,

One of my earliest memories is of Harpers Ferry.

That is a town that I am sure you know well, as it was from there that John Brown mounted his failed October 15, 1859,[1] uprising that was among the factors that led to the Civil War, which officially began on April 12, 1861, (as you already know) when Confederate troops fired on Fort Sumter in South Carolina and the Union troops surrendered.

My memory of Harpers Ferry is of watermelon.

It was the 1950s and I had to be around 5 years old. My father took me on a trip to Harpers Ferry from our home in Arlington, Virginia.

We visited an old hotel that had a patio overlooking the Potomac Water Gap. We were dining on that patio when the waiter – a Black man wearing a bow tie and whom my father respectfully called sir – asked if I wanted salt on my watermelon. I was shocked by the question. I had never heard of such a thing, but later learned that it is a delicacy that many enjoy.

I have no idea why that moment stands out. Little makes sense to me about how the brain works. Strange and minute memories sometimes stand out while important and monumental moments are sometimes pushed into the recess of our mind.

You might be confused as to why I am writing to you.

You obviously did not write your letters to me.

You wouldn't have written any letters to me.

You were killed in what became known as the Battle of Gettysburg generations before I was born.

But we are family.

---

1   John Brown was an abolitionist who hoped a raid on the federal arsenal at Harpers Ferry would lead to a slave rebellion. He was captured and hung but considered a martyr to his cause.

I am Benjamin Kendrick Buckley, your nephew's grandson. That means that you are my great-grand uncle. I would like to refer to you as my Uncle Chris for the remainder of our correspondence.

Your younger brother, William Thomas Kendrick, had a son named Benjamin Burks Kendrick who was born in 1884 in Woodland, Georgia, which is in the same county, Talbot, where you were born. Burks, as people called him, was the last of your brother's six children and was a real go getter. He earned a Ph.D. from Columbia University, became a professor of history, and wrote a book called *The Journal of the Joint Committee of Fifteen on Reconstruction (39th Congress, 1865-1867)*.

Benjamin Burks Kendrick was named after your father, obviously, and it seems the family loves the name Benjamin because it was also passed down to your brother, Benjamin Calloway Kendrick, to your nephew and then to me.

I am the son of Janet Kendrick Buckley, who was the fifth child of Benjamin Burks Kendrick, the historian.

But your spirit may already know all of this.

Perhaps we have met before; if we have not, we are meeting now.

In 2019, I retired from my job as a building inspector for the City of Tampa and purchased a modest home in Harpers Ferry. My sweetheart and I love the wildlife and the historical nature of the town of less than 300 residents.

During an extended stay there in 2020, I decided to find out if my historian grandfather had written anything about the town. That search led me to the University of North Carolina, where they have a file under my grandfather's name. But he did not write anything in that file. Instead, per chance, I found a file under the Kendrick name, it was full of your letters to your family, written from the front lines of the bloodiest war in U.S. history.

Apparently, your family saved the letters and passed them down. My grandfather then donated them to the university for safekeeping.

After reading through the letters, as a tribute to your life, I was emotionally compelled to visit the site of your death in Gettysburg.

I was surprised and anxious to have made this accidental discovery. After all, I was told truly little about you from my mother, Janet. I told my life-partner my discovery. She too was overwhelmed.

After reading through the letters together, as a tribute to your life, we made the trip to the Gettysburg National Military Park.

We packed the car for a two-day trip and drove off to discover what I could about my newly found relative. This was a visit during a global pandemic, known as the COVID-19 Pandemic. The Park's Visitor Center and other points of interest were closed; however, driving, biking, or walking through was allowed. Day one of our visit to the Park we walked various locations. A gracious guide, in training, whom we met on a path alongside the Wheatfield Battlefield volunteered to show us the location of the Georgia Infantry Monument. The three of us walked on a narrow asphalt road, into the woods towards the plaque.

The woods were quiet, as no other tourists were present. The still, crisp Autumn day was interrupted by the sound of rustling leaves on the forest floor. The guide stated, "Oh don't be surprised; there are deer that may run through, so be mindful." My partner began to drop back more as the disturbance became closer, and louder. I too, slowed, and turned to my right, because the noise was in fact growing stronger. My partner and I thought, "Boy, this is going to be several deer coming through, or maybe not a deer, but a bear!" We all stopped. My partner pulled her camera phone out to snap a wildlife photo to show our friends back home. What a deer sighting this would be!

The noise now had appeared at the edge of the trees. To our astonishment there was no wildlife. It was a spinning turbine of fallen leaves, spinning like a tiny tornado toward us! It hovered over the ground about 3-4 feet in height, and about 2- 3 feet in diameter, propelled by a gust of wind conjured up from an invisible force. We stood mesmerized and puzzled as the whirlpool of leaves moved towards us. It spun and spun, it reached halfway, then stopped; as if it was looking at us, acknowledging us, as if to greet us. It crossed the paved road before us and continued to the opposite side, up a small incline. And, like taking a large inhale of breath; the leaves fluttered upward, and then exhaled that breath, the leaves fell one by one to the ground, peacefully underneath a large tree.

My partner took pictures. Emotions ran high. Shaking with tears in her eyes, she turned to me and said, "That was Chris. That was

H.C. He came to show you where he lies." She said this to me because I had become upset after learning what had become of most of the Confederate Soldiers that died after their army retreated from the three days of battle. We have been searching for your grave marker, to no avail. We both felt at that moment we found you. And at that moment, "I had to Remember You!"

Maybe I'm crazy.

Maybe it was just nature, and am I now writing letters to a spinning turbine of leaves?

I believe it was you.

Finding your letters was kismet. It is what I needed in my life.

I discovered them at a time when I am dealing with my own internal civil war.

Receive my love, for I now welcome yours.

Benjamin Kendrick Buckley

LETTER 2

Darksville Va.

July 5th, 1861

Dear father and family,

Having been absent from home some considerable length of time, I feel like writing, but I must be as brief as possible, for my time is short.

We are here in camps at Darksville expecting a fight every moment or on order to that effect. We were pushed off here in a force march having only 3 hours to pack up and be in line and also we had to leave our knapsacks and every thing that we could do with out. We, night before. And last night cooked the most of our victuals on a rock. Some few had a frying pan.

The reason that we were driven off here in such hast, we got the news that our men were driven back by the enemy which was the fact they were not strong enough for the enemy's force. They retreated back some miles and camped at which place we found them that night.

Notwithstanding all our lacking we have gotten about 60+ Yankees for prisoners. We got them on picket guard among whom to your astonishment was also John Brown's brother. You may not think so, but I saw all of them my-self. Surgeon Brown[1] says that he was in the engagement which old John Brown made in 1859 and would have been with his brother but would not get ready in time to meet him. O Sir, he acknowledged frankly that he is no friend to the South. He says that he is [in] the South to get old Va. back where she belongs, but I hardly think he will not succeed.

We get some 3 or 4 every day. Last night we got 4. Today 3. And looking now for 11. So says our picket we met 41 Yankees day before yesterday between Winchester and this place who

---

1   Surgeon was likely his title and not his name. It is unclear which of John Brown's brother this could have been.

were the meanest looking men that I ever saw in my life. I assure you that if you were to see them you would say the same.

My time is out. I am called out to be ready for orders at any moment.

Father, please excuse me for doing no better in writing than I have. I am well but about 10 of our men are sick now. You need not write to me for in 2 hours I may be in line of battle.

Your affectionate son,
H. C. Kendrick

N.B.[2] give my love to all the family and friends about there. Remember me.
Where we expect the fight is at Martinsburg.

---

2   Nota Bene, is a Latin phrase for "note well" and once regularly used in correspondence appearing c. 1711 to call attention to a specific detail.

LETTER 2 REPLY

Dear H.C.,

Your war remains the bloodiest in United States history with more than 620,000 Americans killed.

The bloodiest in my lifetime was the Vietnam War with more than 58,000 Americans killed.

Vietnam was also the first televised war. Each night, I sat in my living room with my parents, staring at the television and receiving updates. Those updates typically framed the war as though we were winning easily and with limited casualties.

The news anchor would tell of a great battle in North Vietnam and cite and declare that the North Vietnamese suffered mass casualties while the United States came out relatively unscathed. That always struck me as odd. By day, families would weep because a loved one had died in battle. By night, a trusted news anchor with a smile told me there were no casualties.

"Remember me."

Of all your letters, of all the lines you wrote, that one stands out the most to me.

"Remember me."

You believed you were only hours from battle and obviously wondered if you would make it back alive. You were willing to die because the Yankees *"were the meanest looking men"* you *"ever saw"* in your life.

Oh, I am sure there were some very mean Yankees, just as there were some very mean Confederates. And just as you knew many kind Confederates, there were many kind Yankees.

Mostly, those on both sides of that war were like you – normal, everyday men willing to pick up a weapon to battle the enemy whom their leaders have told them were "very mean."

In your first letter, you told your father that "*the new Confederate government is a good friend of ours.*"

Many years after you died, the United States elected Ronald Reagan as president. He was a former actor whose colorful personality and superb oratory skills made him one of the most popular presidents in U.S. history. Among his more famous lines was, "*The nine most terrifying words in the English language are: 'I'm from the government, and I'm here to help.'*"

President Reagan believed in a small federal government, meaning he preferred that the private sector take on as many responsibilities as possible because he believed that the government's bureaucracy and fallibility make things worse.

He also believed individuals in leadership positions within the government often lead in ways that benefit them rather than the masses.

That is often the cause of war.

I wonder, besides losing the handful of enslaved persons working your plantation, how would staying part of the United States have hurt your family? From what I can tell, losing those enslaved persons or having to pay them for their work would hardly have had much of a negative impact on your cotton plantation in Talbot County's Pleasant Hill. Was that worth dying over? Your father understood that. Its why family history is so adamant that he did not believe in the Civil War and preferred to free his enslaved and stick with the Union.

But the Confederacy had you convinced that the war was also about separating from those evil Yankees.

You wrote that you met the captured brother of John Brown. But John Brown did not have a brother named Surgeon. Perhaps you meant he had a brother who was a surgeon. But I have not read he had a brother in such a field. Perhaps he was a brother in the religious sense, a brother of his congregation, a brother to his cause. Perhaps, you believed a lie.

You believed the Yankees were all evil.

The Vietnam War was fought to prevent communism from spreading into South Vietnam. Communism, we are taught in the United States, is evil and we must do all we can to defeat it.

North Vietnam won the war and, today, the entire nation is unified under "evil communism." Vietnam is also a friendly trading partner of the United States. Go figure.

* * *

As I mentioned in the previous letter, we are related through your brother William Thomas Kendrick, whose son was my grandfather, Benjamin Burks Kendrick.

Your brother, of course, also fought in the Civil War, making my grandfather the son of a man who battled the evil Yankees.

My grandfather graduated from Mercer University in Georgia. He then met my grandmother, Elizabeth Shields, from Hudson, New York, who was teaching at a high school in Columbus, Georgia.

When my grandfather decided to further his education and earn a Ph.D., he chose Columbia University in New York for two reasons:

1. It was and remains a fine institution of higher learning.

2. It allowed my grandmother to be closer to her family who lived in the nearby borough of Queens, in New York City, where she was raised.

Yes, H.C., the son of your Confederate veteran brother married a Yankee, went to New York to live, and raised three children who were born Yankees.

He realized the North was not cart blanche evil.

Had you lived, you too would likely have been OK with such a union with the Union.

One more bizarre fact about our family.

When my grandfather died, I am told, the Secret Service was at his deathbed. My mother was not sure why. Or maybe she just did not think I should know. I often wonder what else was kept from me and if or how it was connected to what happened to me as a child.

But I am getting ahead of myself.

I am not ready to discuss that yet.

Your affectionate nephew who will not forget you,

Benjamin

LETTER 3

July 18th, 1861

Dear brother,

Now after 9.O. clock P.M. I take my seat to let you know that I am as before, old Mos Tither[1]. I tell you old Mos Tit. is in a fair way of fattening now. I know this sounds familiar to you, Johnnie, and Binnie.

I know that you, that father, and mother think that this is vain in me, but I write it merely to be social and to remind you of former times. Thommie I would like to have some of your good old June apples about now I tell you. You may think that I am joking, but I tell you old fellow I would, the best in the world. Oh show, I am too foolish for a man of my station. I will stop this nonsense now.

Well brother I am left here now to take care of the sick that are in the private houses, and also to superintend those that are in the hospital. Out of about thirty thousand there are about 15,000 soldiers including the militia too. And to tell you the truth about one half of the latter are yankees both by birth and principle. I would not trust them out of my sight.

The report is, that old Gen. Beauregard[2] was fighting at Manassas Junction and was about to be defeated. He sent for assistance, to Johnston[3] and that is the reason that there are no more troops here than are now. And as I am the sec. [secretary] of the company, I have to be left behind. Which I do not like at all. I want to be in all the fights that ever are in the

---

1   A tither is someone who collects parishioner donations for the church, but it is unclear to what this is referring.

2   Gen. Pierre Gustave Toutant-Beauregard, more commonly known as Gen. G.T. Beauregard, is perhaps best known for leading the attack on Fort Sumter on April 12, 1861, which is considered the start of the Civil War.

3   Gen. Albert Sidney Johnston was considered the Confederate Army's top officer until Gen. Robert E. Lee emerged. He died early in the war, on April 6, 1862, during the Battle of Shiloh.

war. I think Thom., that I shall kill a yankee before I get back yet.

Now since I have been writing, I have heard that Beauregard has taken Alexandria but do not believe a word of it. And also heard that he was throwing [bombs] into the city of Washington; but I do not believe one single word of any of it. So, you may just believe, as the old saying is, your part of it.

Don't take to heart what I say about it, for I give it for what it is worth. Just let me relate a circumstance to you that will make you exercise your own judgement about anything you may hear: that is this, we were lying quietly as a people could, in camps about 2 weeks ago and the news came to us very directly apparently, that the yankees had surrounded Gen. Jonston [Johnston] and his army, and had them in strings. There is nothing of it neither is there any prospect of it.

I must say that I do not like our Gen. at all, for he is too much disposed to give back from the yankees. I'll tell you just how he is, he, the very st. [first] idea he has of a fight, begins to devise some plan by which he may get away, and we do not like that at all. A great many of the soldiers, as well as myself, have come to the conclusion that he is about as much for the man with whom, apparently he is contending as, for the southerners. And not only the soldiers, but the people of Winchester also believe the same thing.

Thommie I want you to write to me, as soon as you can, and let me hear how you are getting along at home with the farm and other things that pertain thereto. Thomas I am getting along the best you ever saw in your life, but I would not advise you to leave Ma. and Pa. there by them-selves, but you must [stay] and take care of them.

If you do not think that without fighting, you can enjoy the liberty gained by the confederate troops, why when I get home I, of course as a brother, will share with you. And if you think that a share of my joy will not do you why I will let you have it all sometimes to pasify you.

20

Brother it is getting late and for the present I rekon it will be the best for me to close, but I feel like I could write all night to you about the war. But as I am getting hoarse I will stop directly.

Brother, my health is better than it has been in any part of my life, I am getting as fat as a pig in the pin well fed with old Georgia corn. I enjoy my time the best in the world. Patriotism glows within my heart rapidly as the sun runs. Old Va. never tire.

Give my love to all the family and receive a large portion for your-self.

Good by my lovely brother.

Your loving brother,

H. C. Kendrick Sec.

N.B. consign your letter to H.C. Kendrick 9 Regiment Georgia volunteers in care of Capt. P.S. Morris. Without pooting any place but Va. and I will get it sure.

P.S. tell Ma that I have been a good boy since I left home, and expect to be as long as I am in the army and longer too. Ma. and sister Lizzie and sister Sallie, my best respects to you. My heart grows with love for you. Remember me all of you.

O yes, I have gotten to be a first rate cook. When I get home I intend to make you some biscuits and let you judge for your-self. Then if you no like em, you no take em.

LETTER 3 REPLY

Dear H.C.

My parents sent me to all sorts of summer camps when I was a little kid. I would spend a week at one, two weeks at another, and so on, each in different cities and states.

One in Vermont had a particularly peculiar custom.

They had set up an elevated boxing ring alongside the road every Saturday. They then broke up some of the campers by age and size, of which I was one on quite a few occasions and gave us each a pair of gloves and headgear and had us duke it out for three rounds.

That is not what is peculiar. This is: It took place in the evening with lights illuminating the ring. The camp then had bleachers set up so that the campers and townspeople could watch.

Think about that: For a full summer, the campers beat on one another for the amusement of the locals. Bizarre.

I tell you that story because it hit me that you wrote that last letter just three days before the Battle of Manassas, considered the first major battle of the war. You are of course supposed to participate, but a train accident stops you and your fellow soldiers from doing so. (You mentioned that in your next letter. I read ahead.)

That battle is also particularly peculiar.

The northerners were certain that the Union Army would win that battle in such a decisive manner that the war would be instantly over. So, well-to-do Washingtonians packed picnic baskets and hiked to the countryside to watch the battle.

As you later learned, it did not turn out the way the northerners predicted. They were the ones who lost in a decisive manner and the picnickers watched as the Union soldiers ran by them in retreat.

There are stories of senators screaming at the soldiers to go back and fight.

You wrote to your brother, "Patriotism glows within my heart rapidly as the sun runs."

Those Union soldiers were equally patriotic. They too marched into battle for the cause their leaders put before them.

But what about those leaders - those who funded the big businesses impacted by the government, those who gave large sums of money to elected officials who supported their vision for the nation, and those elected to carry out those visions? Did they show patriotism as they watched the battle? Absolutely not. They showed their true colors as they watched the battle without getting involved when things became ugly. They were willing to send others to their deaths for their cause but were not willing to die for it themselves.

I tell you this story so that you do not think I am against only the South. I wonder if my last letter came off like that.

I am against both sides.

Would I trust your Confederate leaders? No.

But I would not trust the Union leaders either.

I do not fully trust any government, past or present.

Governments seem too willing to send young men, and today, young women, and more correctly young people, to their deaths.

* * *

For the record, I stayed at that Vermont camp for three or four weeks and won all my fights. I had good hands.

Years later, when I was around 22, I was hanging out with a friend who was one of the biggest and certainly the toughest guys I knew. He was so tough that he later joined a motorcycle club, which, for a while, was a notorious group of outlaws.

I noticed a pair of boxing gloves hanging on the wall and challenged him to a "friendly" bout.

A few friends were with us, and we all went outside for the "friendly" fight. I knew he was stronger – he outweighed me by at least 100 lbs. – but I had more boxing skill. This was not a street fight. I noticed that, as he danced around me, he allowed his legs to cross. So, I peppered him with a jab. It was not a hard punch, but, because I timed it to land when his legs were crossed, he lost balance, fell backwards, and slammed his head into the ground. Our friends started laughing, which infuriated him, so he leapt up and cracked me so hard in the jaw that my head spun, and I fell, out cold, to the ground.

He won.

I saw him the next day.

I had a nice hangover from the punch.

But he was far from unscathed. His head was pounding too.

The Union suffered around 3,000 casualties at the Battle of Manassas in their loss.

The Confederacy "only" had 1,750 in "victory."

Your loving nephew,

Ben

LETTER 4

Manassas, Va.

August 8th, 1861

Dear father,

Having taken down some dots and circumstances of my travels in this country and in fact ever since I left home, with the greatest pleasure seat my-self to write them to you.

In the first place, we came to Richmond, in which place we were mustered in the service of the Confederate states for or during the term of the war, which we did with perfect clarity and cheerfulness not only that, but with eagerness.

After having stayed there a few days then we went to Manassas Junction at which place we arrived about 2 P.M. and remained until about 8 A.M. After which we started from this noble and magnificent place - well fortified with breast works - batteries well mounted and placed thereon. So I think that we are prepaired to meet the enemy at that place to Strasburg. And on the way we saw many beautiful and magnificent sceneries, which charmed our eyes and opened our imagination. One of which, was the valley below which presented a fine scope of trees and flours - above tremendous rocks, apparently ready to fall down on us, yet firmly fixed there.

Strasburg is one of the most beautiful places that I ever saw - situated between two branches of the Alleganies, upon the charming Shenandoah river, it has a varied excellency seldom surpassed by any place. The diversifications are many - scattered with many beautiful farms on the north side of it - the fine and noble mountains stretching on the east and west. Going southward in wavy exuberance, all unite to make the scenery more beautiful. Now the ride stops.

Well, boys, said the Col., let us take it a foot.

Well, said the boys, we are ready and anxious to go so we can have a fight with the yankees.

So - on the morning of the 28th of June, we took the line of march for Winchester which we found to our astonishment, to be very pleasant. We did not march more than 8 or 10 miles per day which did not hurt us of course. However we had a few sick men in the regiment, who did not stand it so well. But with that exception, we got along well, much better than you might expect of boys who never saw a musket before. We were attached to Bartow's Brigade[1] - went into camp in a most excellent oak grove about one, or one-and-a quarter miles from town.

Late in the afternoon of the 4th day after our arrival to Winchester, news came to us stating that the Federal troops were in Martinsburg and were advancing on us about 22 miles from this place. Soon after we got the news which was about 3 P.M. we took the line of march in that direction, and went out from here about 5 miles. At which place we bivouaced all night. Rather unpleasant it was too. Soon the next morning after the sun beamed his light upon us, we left there and made our way in the direction of Martinsburg. On our way there, we met 41 yankees, among whom was one commissioned officer. Their hands were all tied. They looked hopeless - moved with reluctance and sorrow. They said their time had nearly expired. But fortunately for them we got them. For from what I can learn, they would have been in a worse condition than they are, had we not got them.

Father I hear frequently that they are starving in the north every day. I am glad of it too. For they ought not to have come over here in old Va. to fight us. We will give them sort yet.

After having advanced to within a few miles of Martinsburg, then occupied by the enemy, we halted and unfolded in line of battle. The post, assigned to our portion of the army,

---

1   Led by Col. Francis Bartow, a former United States representative who was part of the Georgia militia. He died in the First Battle of Manassas.

was an old wheat field, upon which the sun threw all his powers of heat. At which place we bivouaced 4 days with a full determination to fight. We could frequently hear the enemy were advancing on us and would be arranged in line of battle for to await them with balls and give them a warm reception. Well, we are on the old wheat field yet, not any battle. But at every point, war, war, war, war would salute our ears. Our head did ring with news bringing as I and all the rest thought, would bring about a fight.

The 4th night after our arrival at Darkesville we received orders to prepare for a battle. We were all awakened by touch they were not allowed to call us loud enough to be heard more than 10 feet. Now thought we that a fight would come sure. While up, we were not allowed to kindle a fire for any purpose at all. Notwithstanding, we expected a fight I could hear more laughing remarks made use of than ever before. Well morning came on, and the sun burst forth in his charming beauty - defying the power of man to quench his shining powers and stop his shooting rays, and no battle yet.

But alas! Alas! We had to retreat from Darkesville becaus the enemy was about to surround us, as we were badly situated geologically. We were geologically in an acute angle. They had superior numbers consequently we thought it best to fall back to Winchester. Well we fell back to Winchester at our former camp - stayed there some two or three days, then in a great hurry were moved to within about 400 yards of Winchester north thereof. At which place we did not expect any difficulty at all, and did not have one.

We stayed there 2 days and were hurried off to some point, we did not know where, nor did we care, for we came here to fight and intend to do it if there is not peace made in some other way, which I think is very probable now. But again; we found the [secrete] after a while.

We waded the Shenandoah River about 12 o clock in the night and went on to Piedmont and on account of the collision of the cars we did not get off to Manassas in time for the fight.

Dear father I am sitting out in the woods writing on my knee. Consequently you cannot expect much. I could tell you a great-deal about my travels, but have not the time and convenience and paper. But I will write again, if nothing prevents me. I have a bad chance to write you. I am well and fat as a pig and a little saucy, but not contemptuously so. I have gotten along as well as any body could have gotten along in the world. Tell sister Sarah I would like the best in the world to see her little daughter. Give my love to all the family and to friends around there.

Family, brother R.S. brother, Jos. William, all my sisters and brothers.

Tell them that I will write to them as soon as I can. You and Ma must write to me sure if no one else. [Go] it sister E. I shall expect to get a few ideas from you when I get back home you must hold your-self in readiness. I shall call on you. All write that can.

You dear loving son,

H. C. Kendrick

Brother R.S. you and brother W.T. must write as soon as you can. I have written to you both. Don't forget me but think of the cause in which I am engaged.

N.B. tell Ma. that I will write to her the next. Ma. don't think strange of me, for when I write to one I intend it for all.

LETTER 4 REPLY

Dear H.C.

We moved six times during my childhood. We never moved far. Each new home was always within a few miles of the other, always in the shadow of the Pentagon in Arlington, Virginia.

My parents made side money in real estate. They would purchase a home, fix it up and then sell it or, as they say in the business, flip it.

My earliest memory is of the home on 18th Street. A few blocks away was an old house that someone converted into a neighborhood convenience store. It's where kids took loose change that they'd found, earned, or were given by adults to purchase sodas, ice cream, and candy. Adults frequented it for milk, bread, cigarettes, and other small items. My mother loved, loved, loved candy bars primarily, Hershey's Chocolate. She'd walk to the store, wait until she was home to open the candy bar, and then sit back and enjoy every morsel of it while relaxing in her favorite chair.

A brickyard was near the Pentagon and only a short drive from our home. When the brickyard shut down, my parents hurried over for the going out of business sale. Those bricks were used to finish some projects performed at that house, and some were saved for the next house. It was about 1957 and we moved soon after to our 3rd location.

Among the more memorable of the homes was located on 24th Street. It was a large home split into four apartments with us living in the basement apartment and my parents renting the remaining three. A family of five lived directly across the street. They had three children, each was older than me, with the eldest of the three and in high school by the time we met. They were three tough brothers who liked to playfully tease me. The middle one called me silly names like Benji Stingy and told his mother crazy lies, such as that I liked to walk the neighborhood to find girls bicycle seats to sniff.

As a child my focus of that neighborhood was the nearby Potomac Yards, a tremendous series of train tracks that ran for miles alongside U.S. Highway 1, perhaps the busiest highway on the east coast. It was home to a Hobo Jungle where the homeless slept. It was covered in junk and litter, rats scurried about. Yet, it was the most wonderful place I had ever seen and, have ever seen.

I am struck by your descriptions of the beautiful landscapes that you saw. Even as you marched all those hard miles and prepared for a battle that could take your life and the lives of your friends, you took the time to appreciate the world.

> *Strasburg is one of the most beautiful places that I ever saw.*
>
> *Situated between two branches of the Alleghenies, upon the charming Shenandoah River, it has a varied excellency seldom surpassed by any place. The diversifications are many, scattered with many beautiful farms on the north side of it, the fine and noble mountains stretching on the east and west. Going southward in waves of exuberance, all unite to make the scenery more beautiful.*

You were a warrior, yet also a poet.

I believe such an approach is necessary to make it through life, whether that is a life at war, or a life with only small issues that seem large.

Moving a lot prevented me from having long lasting friendships. I could still ride my bike a short distance to visit the kids from my former neighborhoods, but I could never be as close with them as they were with each other. They were neighbors. That is a different bond. I was forever an outsider.

But, when I was at that railroad yard, the boys were not separated by neighborhoods. We were one collective unit, all coming together for a great adventure, an adventure that always stopped my mind from dwelling on anything bad.

Some days we'd just watch the trains arrive and depart. For us, the sound of the boxcars rumbling down the tracks and blowing their whistles was like the sound of evening crickets in the suburbs or waves on the beach.

We'd of course have treasure hunts. Hobos would hide belongings everywhere and then leave some behind when they would depart for another town. And packages being delivered via train would sometimes get left behind in the confusion of the day. We'd never find anything that was real treasure, but discovering an old tool, a Canadian coin, or an unopened box of books, felt like a map had just led us to pirate booty.

And when my friend wasn't busy telling people that I smelled girl's bicycle seats, we made real booty from that railroad yard. Hobos and railroad workers would finish off a drink and leave the bottle behind on the ground. We'd collect as many as we could, tossing each in a basket, and then bring them to the neighborhood corner store, where the owner gave us two cents a bottle. On most days we went that route, we'd likely find 10 bottles between us, earning a whopping 10 cents apiece, enough for one piece of candy only. But it was never about the money. It was always about the adventure.

We were eventually banned from bringing bottles to that store. We learned that the owner took our bottles and then stored them out back in the alley to be recycled. So, we'd bring him bottles, wait an hour, sneak behind the store to retrieve them, and then bring the same bottles back to him for more money. That worked a few times before he caught on and reamed us good.

Other childhood memories of the old neighborhood come to mind. I will now tell you of my own internal civil war that I mentioned in my first letter. I did not feel it was appropriate to mention in my first letter so I will tell you now. When I was about 6 years old, I suffered something I would never wish on my worst enemy.

I was raped by an adult male.

It didn't destroy my life as such a tragedy has done to so many other lives. I pushed through the pain and overcame it. I have a family, raised my son, who has become a doctor with a family of his own. I worked throughout my life, and I was able to retire after earning modest wealth through my efforts.

Yet, I often think about that horrific day. I wonder why it happened. Was it a random act? Or was I deliberately targeted by the government? I know that sounds crazy, but I can explain, please listen, and hear me. Just as it is difficult to tell the story in full, it is hard to write it. So please give me the time that I need. It's easier to tell in bits and pieces than in full.

If your spirit is still here on earth, there is likely a reason. Some believe a spirit remains on earth when they still have a mission to complete here.

Maybe, you are still here for me. Maybe, I am your mission.

Maybe, you are meant to assist me. Maybe, only someone who has endured the cruelty of a civil war can help me to understand my civil war.

I don't expect you to reply to these letters through some spiritual manner. I just need someone with whom to talk. I just need someone upon whom to unload all that is running through my head.

You appeared to me in those woods for a reason. Perhaps, this is why.

Through my replies to your letters, you can be a figurative shoulder on which for me to lean.

I'd like to try.

The sexual assault I suffered was also always in the back of my mind when I was a child. You cannot learn to cope with such a tragedy until you understand it. No child can understand something that horrific. But I was always at peace when at that railroad yard.

The Shenandoah River Valley helped you make it through your Civil War. It became your place of peace.

That railroad yard helped me through mine.

It's funny how the mind works.

Your dear loving nephew,

Ben

LETTER 5

Manassas Junction

August 16th, 1861

Dear brother,

Having been out from the nois of the boys of the camp, I with perfect composure seat my-self to write to you. Brother, I have not writen to you before from the fact that I been so busily engaged that I could not. And I have written to Pa and brother R.S. and Thomas, and to several of my friends, and have not received a letter yet, only the one that Pa sent by Mr Chaney. That is the only one I have received from home yet.[1]

Dear brother I am in fine health, my task is easy, my burden light, and my condition good. The health that I enjoy in the company is not found in all. We have a good many sick in the regiment. I think that some of the companies that have been mustering 70 or 80, now muster 40 to 45. Sickness prevails through this country. I thank God that I have been well all the time. You may think that I say that I have been well just to keep you all from being uneasy about me, but not so. I have been well ever since I have been in old Va. In fact I have fattened all the time. Now I will close about that, I have I been writing.

Brother, tell Pa to send me some winter clothing. I want one coat, not a round about, but long tail coat. I want a pair of pants, a pair or two of socks, 2 pair of drawers, and some paper and ink in the box. And also, some pens to write with.

Dear brother I would like the best in the world. You have no idea how I would enjoy seeing her. Write to me what you are going to name her. Give her a good name and let her have the raising corresponding therewith.

---

1   H.C. is now approximately four months into this war, and notedly has only received one letter from home. From the Collections of Letters the author has, H.C. appears to have written home already seven times.

Now brother I will tell you something about the war. We hear a [great deal] about the war. We can hear almost any thing we wish. We heard the other day that there was a fight in Va. in which, we lost 800 men. We did not learn how many of the enemy that were killed. We heard, however, that we took all of their waggons and horses, and stated also the paper, that would come that would give the number of the yankees that were killed.

I now must close. Write soon.

Give my love to all the family.

Yours fraternally,

H. C. Kendrick

Brother, I have not got ten cents in change therefore you will have to pay for this letter your-self. I hate to send a letter unpaid for but cannot help it this time.

N.B. be sure you write to me, and let me hear the news that you get there in old Ga. I do not get any Ga. papers, and consequently, cannot tell anything about what is going on there. Tell Pa to send me thos cloths, and Ma to send me thos socks and drawers.

May God bless you all there while I am fighting here for my country. Then after the victory shall have been won I, will I hope, to be there to enjoy the comforts of home with you.

May God save us all from the darts of the enemy, is my prayer for [selvish] sake.

LETTER 5 REPLY

Dear H.C.,

During World War II, nearly a century after you died in battle, the United States established a secret military base on Ascension Island.

A volcanic island located in the South Atlantic Ocean about 1,000 miles from Africa and 1,400 from Brazil, it was and is still controlled by The United Kingdom, who allowed the United States to build a base and runway there to help win the 2nd World War.

The mainstream story about the island is that the United States uses it as a tracking station by employing radar that can track both friendly and enemy missiles in that region of the world and that can be used to support NASA's space exploration. I wonder, if even from the spirit world, you marvel at man's ability to now explore space, or do spirits see things far more wondrous?

There have long been rumors that the island was and is still used to spy on friends and foes by eavesdropping on their conversations via top secret technology.

I can't speak to whether the eavesdropping or missile tracking is true, but I can tell you from firsthand experience that the radar stories are.

Anyway, I worked on Ascension Island in the late-1980s as a carpenter, hired by a government contractor to help build barracks for workers who are stationed on the island.

It was one of the most beautiful places I have ever been. At night, without any light pollution for 1,000 miles or more in every direction, I could see every star in the sky. It must have been how the sky looked during your lifetime, before mankind lit up the world.

It was nearly impossible to reach the island uninvited, but we often had invited guests from governments and militaries from all over the world. As a laborer, I was told to keep my head down and to stay out of whatever business was going on there.

But one day, an American woman – I can't recall if she was military or government – visited. She had a little too much to drink that night and invited a few of the laborers to check out what she was working on.

So, she drove us to a mountain on a part of the island that I was not aware of, where there was a hanger filled with machinery. She led us to a particular machine that was outside the hangar and loudly humming. She warned us to not step in front of it because it was shooting invisible lasers into space. I looked up and, maybe 20 or 30 feet above our heads, could see faint traces of the lasers exposed by humid mist.

Then she took us inside the hanger to show us a small jet. It had a glass nose and could fit two men - a pilot and a second man who laid in the front of the jet to operate a different laser. After showing us the jet, she pointed to a hill about a mile away and said there is another laser machine set up.

The woman told us the three lasers were being used to track and map the stars. It was part of our nation's Star Wars Program, a proposed missile defense system in space. She called it Star Stepping.

Imagine all that.

I cannot imagine what you think of all this as you watch the world from beyond the grave.

I'm glad to read that you were wary of the news you heard about the war. Yes, you can hear anything that you wish, but you seemed to know that was different from hearing the truth.

I am also glad that your health was well, but sad to hear that many others could not say the same. And I wonder if your government even cared. Did they want those young men nursed back to health because they cared for their wellbeing or because they needed them to serve as bullet catchers for their "great cause?"

I'm sure that by now you are wondering what birthed my great distrust for government.

There are many reasons, one of which involves Ascension Island and something as basic as my health.

I hurt my shoulder while operating a hammer drill to drill into concrete. The constant vibrations were bothering my joints and bones. I figured they'd show me to a doctor, he'd give me some aspirin, tell me to take a few days off and all of my medical expenses would be covered through a workman's compensation claim.

That's not how it went.

My injury would not be covered under a workman's compensation claim.

I asked how that was fair. I'm an American Citizen, I said, and they were supposed to cover my medical costs because I was hurt on the job.

My boss explained that we were not in America, so they didn't need to abide by any of the United States' laws.

I was nothing more than a worker to them and easily replaceable. If I was too hurt to work, they'd find another man to do my job. If I died there, I doubt they'd have cared either. They would have just shipped my body in a box back to the United States on the same plane that had just flown in my replacement.

I worked through it, and as instructed, kept my head down, and never missed a day.

Yours loving nephew,

Ben.

LETTER 6

Dear sister,

Your letter came, I suppose in dieu time. I do not know whether it did or not, for it was not dated consequently, I cannot say. However, that is immaterial. You may know that I was glad to hear from home. I had nearly despaired of ever getting a letter from any of you. One more week would have confirmed me in such a course.

Sister I am in the most beautiful place you ever saw in your life. I, now, am in sight of 17 encampments, about 15,000 men. I can see all over the whole country for 20 miles. One point, can see 60 miles. So, you may know that it is something enchanting, attractive, and fascinating. But alas! Alas! For the rights of this pretty country to be secured, shall demand the blood of the inhabitants thereof.

Well, there is one consolation if they do, why they are worth it. There was a little battle not a great distance from here a few days ago. Not anything like a great fight. But we think that there will be a great battle fought at or near Alexandria before long or a spirit of peace will prevail, one or the other.

But sister I do not think this regiment will be in it, if it comes; for we are situated 2 miles from the Junction for the protection thereof.

Sister you said you had vacation, and would resume again on Monday, furthermore said, that you did not know whom you would have there to instruct you and help write compositions- seem to think that you were disfurnished an instructor in a great measure. But you are not, from the fact that self reliance and dependence are productive of much tallent and intelligence.

I know sis, that I am missed at home very much and am wanting there, but the caus for which I am here is that, by which you live pleasantly and peacefully in this world and if it is not accomplished why you see that at once, ruin and sorrow; desolation and misery; would be the consequences. Well I resume my old topic.

Sis I, if peace was made, would like the best in the world to be there to impart to you instruction, but as it is, I am not anxious to be there.

Though I often think of my old desk and lamp by which I used to sit at night and study for improvement, but now it is so, that I have to study only my old bible, that good old book, out of which I get good information. Notwithstanding I have that good old book to study, I am not satisfied, for I would like to inform my-self in profane history.

Sis, dear sis, how often do I think of thee while in my tent, in which I am now. I read half book in the bible every day.

Sis, my health is exceedingly good. I am as fat as I can be, and equally as saucy. Not in a contemptable manner, but in a filial and friendly way.

Sis since I have been writing, I have stoped and had my gun and knapsack inspected. In which I had the prais for having a clean gun and knapsack.

Sis tell brother R.S. to write to me. Tell sis Sallie Williams, sis Mary Ken. [Kendrick] to write to me. All of you write to me as soon as you can.

Your loving brother,
H. C. Kendrick

LETTER 6 REPLY

Dear H.C.

My parents were very formal.

My father was a military veteran who brought that regimented military style to our household.

One of my chores was to set the table. Each spoon, fork, plate, and napkin had to be arranged in the perfect order, as though we were dining with the Queen of England. My father would often walk into the dining room as I was setting the table and stand over me like a sergeant. If a utensil was placed down crooked to even the slightest degree, he'd reach over my shoulder and straighten it.

My father also often had me practice writing letters. I had to prove I recalled where the return address went and how to write salutations and closings. "And always use a pen," he'd say. "Pencils are for math and for children who scribble scrabble. Writers use pens." I guess we can blame him for this exercise.

Yes, my parents were very formal.

But they were not very affectionate.

Hugs were rare.

I can only recall my father kissing me one time in my life.

I don't think my mom kissed me even once.

I appreciate your words to your brother to not join the war because your mother and father needed protection. Of course, none listened and all five of your brothers and two brothers in-law joined the cause despite your father being against it. You also inform me, as I read your letters, that three cousins fought in the cause.

And I appreciate that you called her your mother, and only your mother, when she was in fact your stepmother.

You might be happy to know that your parents' love story is one passed down to future generations.

Your father, Benjamin Burks Kendrick, literally helped build Talbot County Georgia, arriving there as the community was founded by those who won land in the property lottery. Because he was such a skilled carpenter, he helped build the courthouse, jail and its first church, where he later served as deacon. Your mother, Frances Lloyd Kendrick, was a parishioner at the church. He spotted her in a pew, and it was love at first sight. Following the service, your father rushed to talk with her parents, hoping for an introduction. They offered something even better – an invite to dinner.

As the story goes, your parents barely spoke during that dinner, but neither could take their eyes off the other. A relationship blossomed, they married and had nine children.

She died after your youngest brother, Ben, was born. She never regained her strength following the pregnancy and passed at the young age of 36. You were just a little boy yourself.

Her final words to your father, according to family history, were, "I'm leaving you, my precious, but I know you will do the very best for our helpless little children. I wish I could help you more."

A year later, your father met and fell in love with Ann Trussell, and they married soon after.

It was tough for her. Neither you, nor your siblings accepted her at first. You understandably wanted your biological mother back. But, in time, you accepted her as mom, and well you should. Imagine being willing to parent nine children, none of whom have a blood tie to you. She was a remarkable woman and a heroine.

I can tell by these letters, as you wrote of the gifts that she sent to you, that your second mother truly loved you.

I know you missed your birth mother, but God then sent you a second mother who was just as loving.

The lack of affection between myself and my parents was partially my fault.

My attacker threatened to kill them if I ever told them what happened.

So, like you, I sought to protect my parents and thought the best way to do so was to build a figurative wall between us. If my attacker ever saw us hugging and kissing and loving, I worried, he might go after them.

In retrospect it's silly. But it's how I thought as a kid, and it impacted my relationship with them for my lifetime.

Your loving nephew,

Ben

LETTER 7

Manassas Junction

August 25th, 1861

Dear mother,

Having just written to sister Elizabeth, I shall not have a great deal to write to you. Notwithstanding that, I do not see how I could get a long in peace if I did not write to you my dear mother. I thank God that I have a mother in Georgia in who, I know, will do all for me that a mother can do for a son.

Mother, how did you get your finger cut off? Did you get them cut off cutting off peaches? Ma, I expect you did.

Ma you stated in your letter that you wanted to send me some wine and peaches, and that father thought that it was unnecessary, for he thought that we would have plenty, but not so, for when a man gets any thing here he eats or wears it himself, and the rest may go without. So ma you send them as soon as you pleas[e] to me individually. Then I will get them.

I tell you that every man is for himself here. You may be assured. We do not know each other here. We will fight for each other here, and do it more readily than we would at home, but necessity has brought us to care for self and no one else. Necessity, as well as it is the origin of all inventions, it is the guide to the disposition of people. I am glad that I have a mother to send me such things as they.

Ma, you may think strange of it, but I have not had a peach, nor plum, since I have been in old Va. Neither have I had a water melon nor muskmelon - in fact - no fruit at all. Plenty water melons are here but the price is outrageous consequently, I will not buy them. I deem it nonsense to get them.

Ma I get plenty of butter and molasses and sometimes a chicken, but do not get one particle of fruit. Ma, don't come to the conclusion, because I say that I get no fruit, that I don't get enough to eat. I get plenty to eat and do not have much to do.

Ma, I washed some clothes the other day. I washed 2 shirts, and one pair drawers. Took my camp kettle down to the branch and I tell you I washed them well too. You used to think that I was a first rate boy to help the women when I was at the house, but you have no idea how useful I would be now if I was there. I can cook as good bread as I want to eat any where. In fact I am a cook. But a morsel at your table would be quite a treat to me now I think. To know that ma made it.

Well Ma, I think I will be there by the last of December next. The war cannot last long, because I do not think the two parties can pay the cost. The expenditure, of the South is, per day, about three hundred thousands dollars. And that of the North, about ten hundred thousand dollars. Now if this be the case, how can they stand it? You know they can't.

Ma, I think that two or three more great battles will close the war. Though we may not get home immediately.

Don't be uneasy about me for I will assure you that I will take good care of my-self in body and mind; in caracter and spirit. So be composed and rest easy. I am under the impression that you will hear good news before long.

Ma. you must write soon as you can. I love to read a letter from any of you. I love to hear from old home.

Ma. good by.

Your loving son,

H.C. Kendrick

N.B. I cannot get hold of ten cent pieces to pay the postage. I have the money but not the change. So, you will have to pay the postage your-self.

LETTER 7 REPLY

Dear H.C.,

I have met and known some terrible people in my life – international drug dealers, biker gang members, and, of course, a rapist.

I have stared pure evil in the face.

One friend's father was perhaps what I'd refer to as a street thug. I don't know what sort of everyday crime he committed to pay the bills. I recall he owned a Cadillac and would often be seen selling something from the trunk. I can only guess he was selling stolen goods or drugs.

That friend's father killed a man.

The friend's mother told us the story. They were walking around Georgetown. A Black man was leaning against a wall. And that father, as he walked by the Black man, pulled out a razor blade and slit the man's neck. The Black man grabbed the wound, trying to put pressure on it to stop the bleeding. But the man collapsed dead to the ground. My friend's father did not know the person. He seemed to have done it just so that he could kill and watch the man die.

Perhaps the ugliest person I met was a coworker when I worked on a construction project in Washington D.C. He stated that he was a former Seabee, which is the United States Navy's Construction Battalion (C.B.), hence the "Seabees". They are an arm of the Navy that build and fortify temporary structures needed for battle – bases, bridges, airfields, roads, you name it.

My coworker served in Vietnam and enjoyed regaling me with battle stories, but he more so enjoyed talking about his peaceful stints in the Philippines. He was a real tough, redneck type and would go on and on about fights he was in and prostitutes he bought.

It was odd. We were not close friends and there was nothing about my demeanor that asked for the stories, yet he'd go on and on.

He seemed to think the stories impressed me. He seemed to need to impress me.

Then one day he took it to another level.

He spoke about beating up gay men in the Philippines. He'd seek out a gay man, solicit him and, right after the man performed oral sex on him, my co-worker would beat him into a bloody pulp to "teach him a lesson." I have no idea why he would tell me such a story.

I think about that often.

Initially, I wondered why he didn't see the irony in that. He hated gay men so much that he wanted them all dead yet was partaking in homosexual behavior.

Then, I figured he was probably gay, and he hated himself because of it. Real men aren't gay, he was taught, and he was a real man, so why did he have these feelings, I figured he wondered. So, he fulfilled his desires but then struck out violently at the other man in anger.

But then I realized neither of those are true.

He wasn't ignorant or an angry closeted homosexual.

He was a monster. There is no other way to describe such a man.

There is a lot of ugliness in the world.

There was a lot of ugliness in your world, and you were at the very center of it.

And I wonder, how did you continue to keep such a positive outlook?

You continued to tell your family of the beauty you saw all around you and took great pains to serve as a big brother to your sister rather than worrying more about yourself.

I wonder, did your family and the love you had for them and they for you serve as your strength? Did you wake each morning giving thanks for that love rather than cursing the Lord for dropping you in the middle of a war?

I wish you could write back and help me figure it all out.

Your loving nephew,

Ben.

LETTER 8

August 25th, 1861

Dear brother,

I have eaten dinner, and what a dinner I did have! I made the butter and syrup fly; you may be sure. You know how I used to eat that old black syrup that we had in '59, well, just like I ate that, I eat here, maybe a little more so. I made the best biscuits I have had in some time. Then we had with that good old sheep meat which was just as good as any thing could be.

One of the boys of our mess hollered. Saying, Come up here the 8th Reg. and eat of our mutten, it is just as good as you ever saw in Ga. Come up and eat of it.

Well after a while one of the boys of the Reg. came up, and said, Where is that good old mutten for the 9th Regiment? What do you suppose the reply was that he received? Why it was this, Leave here or wait till we get done, then we will let you have some and not before.

I have often thought of the remarks made at home by the negros when I would hear such as that said. We do not invite a boy here to eat with us unless we think that he has eaten already. We are afraid they may accept of it. When a boy asked for any thing, we do not say help yourself for we are afraid he might do it. And if he did we just politely ask him to keep his hands out of cold victuals, and if he does not do it we lift them out. So you may know how we get along in war.

Thomas, sister E. said in her letter that you wanted to come to war you listen to me, will you? I say I would not come if I was in your place. You had better stay there with mother and father, and take care of them. They need protection, where shall they get it if you come to old Va.? Why they cannot get it and you must stay there. You must not come to the conclusion that you would not be instrumental in gaining the rights of the country, because you are not in the state of old Va. But be reconciled with what you are doing and stay brother.

I have not the time to write any more. I must close. You must write as soon as you can.

Tell John that I would like to see him the best in the world. He must write to me.

> Tell B.C. that he must write to me sure. I want to hear from him. Binnie you must be a good boy and study hard. Make father and mother happy. Tell aunt Sarah to fulfill her promise. Tell her she said she was going to write to me, and has not done it.

Yours fraternally,
H. C. Kendrick

LETTER 8 REPLY

Dear H.C.,

My mother was a bit of a hoarder. Well, that may be harsh, she did save memorabilia – treasures of her life and memories.

She didn't hoard junk or anything like that. She hoarded records.

She died on December 2, 2015, which struck me as odd because that was the day before my birthday. It would have been nice to spend one more with her.

It was also odd because it seems like she predicted it.

Months after she died, I began going through her boxes of records and I found a poem she'd written about her death. She wrote it in 1951, on December 2. Bizarre.

2 AM
2 Dec 1951

So come we now,
as come we must
to lay me down and back to dust.
I'm not to die but only sleep,
and so in sleep my soul departs to give my home a rest.
And after resting all is through
I come again to start my home anew.
— Janet Kendrick Buckley

She also saved these books of S&H green stamps that were given out as rewards at the grocery store. You spent a certain amount, and you'd get a certain number of stamps that were glued into your booklet. Then, when you accumulated enough, you could visit an S&H store and exchange the stamps for something there, small items like candles and bowls and such. S&H went out of business in the 1980s, but mom never did throw out those stamp books. I guess she was hoping for a renaissance.

I've enjoyed reading about your relationship with your mother and, as I wrote earlier, I appreciate that you loved her like she was your biological mother. Blood does not make family. Love makes family. And it is obvious that she loved you and you her.

I know so much about your mothers, but you know so little about mine, who is also your family. She would be your great-niece.

Pages from a diary are among the other items discovered in my mother's box of records.

Perhaps, rather than me telling you about my mother, you would prefer to read her words yourself, almost as though she too is writing to you.

Here are her pages describing her efforts as a civilian working for the government during World War II. Again, another Kendrick Family Member, loyally serving this country. You would be duly proud of her, as am I.

I believe she wrote this in the early 1950s:

> I was born in 1924 in Greensboro, North Carolina, the youngest of four children. My father was a professor of history at the Woman's College of the University of North Carolina from 1923 until 1943.
>
> I went to grammar school and high school at the Curry Training and Demonstration School, which was run by the Women's College UNC.
>
> In 1941, I entered the Women's College and lived in the dormitory on the campus. I had wanted to study physics, but the two professors of physics left the college when the school was started and the physics department sort of collapsed. So, I did not know what to study.
>
> In the middle of my sophomore year, the Curtis Wright Aircraft Corp set up an engineering training program for girls. I entered this program and was sent to Penn State for 10 months of study in aeronautical engineering. This course was concentrated (40 hours of class per week) and amounted to approximately the first two years of engineering school. When I finished this course, I went to Buffalo, N.Y. (This was Jan. 1944.)
>
> For the first six months, I did detailed drafting, but I felt that I wasn't using any mental powers. Then I was transferred to the structures department where I did com-

puting for the vibrations and flutter groups. After I worked with this group for a while, I was given more responsibility and, instead of doing just computing, I carried a job there as a regular engineer and did only the computing necessary for my own project.

The theory of aerodynamics is very complicated and involves higher mathematics. I, of course, did not understand the theory behind the work but realized that mathematics was a very powerful subject and I decided to study it when I went back to college.

At the end of the war, Curtis Wright folded up and I was laid off. I considered going back to Penn State and studying engineering but, because of the large G.I. enrollment and since I was an out of state student, I could not get in right away. So, I went back to the Women's College and studied mathematics. I graduated in 1948.

The David Taylor Model Basin (Navy Department) sent representatives to the Women's College when I was a senior, and I, along with five other girls, were offered jobs in the aerodynamics department. I accepted this job and came to Washington to work. I was not particularly interested in working in Washington and the job did not sound very interesting, but the pay was the best offered when I finished college and five of my friends were coming to work here, so I came.

I did not think the department was organized well at all and so I, and another girl, sent in a beneficial suggestion, which offered a reorganization of the department. It so happened that the reorganization would eliminate our supervisors' jobs. Needless to say, the suggestion did not go over very big and, a couple of weeks later, I was told by my supervisor that there was a job in the hydromechanics department, which I could have. (This was a sort of kick upstairs.)

I took the job eagerly. I was just as glad to leave as they were to have me leave. The beneficial suggestion, which my friend and I offered, was actually very good and now (one-and-a-half years later) they are gradually putting it into effect.

I worked in the aerospace department for two-and-a-half years and disliked the work most of the time as I did just computing and used very little of my mathematics.

Several times during this period I looked for other jobs around town, but I didn't find any that offered much more. I liked most of the people I worked with, so I just stayed on there until I was forced to leave. (Also, I had come to like living in Washington. I did not want to go to a new city.)

When I went to work in the hydromechanics department (still at D.T.M.B.), I worked for a German scientist. I was his only assistant, and we had an office together. Actually, the work wasn't any more enjoyable. It was somewhere different but still mostly computing. I enjoyed working for the German scientist as he was interesting and a kind person. After working for him for a little over a year, he went back to Germany.

I am now working for a rather brilliant and understanding man who is the head of the hydromechanics department. I couldn't ask for a better setup – the only trouble is that I still do computing and still do not like it.

During the last four years, I have decided that I am not really interested in math, physics, or engineering. I have taken 12 hours of courses in math since I finished college and have not enjoyed any of them. I took these courses because I felt that I needed them if I were ever to do anything in math. If I really wanted to be good at my profession, I would have to take about 30 more hours of math and then physics and engineering. And I'm just not interested enough to do this.

Since I've been in the government, I've gotten "excellent" on efficiency ratings, except for the first when I was not very good. People seem to be fairly pleased with my work. I have not had any opportunities to supervise others.

H.C., that marks the end of that entry.

A few things I perhaps should clarify:

Curtis Wright Aircraft Corp produced aircraft for the government. The David Taylor Model Basin developed ships, and my mom, as a human computer, completed complicated math problems for their designs. Over dinner one night she said, *"Did you know I was one of the first computers?"*

As for that German scientist.

I think of him often H.C.

I wonder if that time spent with him had anything to do with what happened to me when I was a boy.

I'll explain more later when I am ready.

I'm getting there.

I'm closer.

I appreciate you providing that shoulder I needed.

Your loving nephew,

Ben

P.S. You wrote, *"Necessity, as well as it is the origin of all inventions, it is the guide to the disposition of people."* That's beautiful.

LETTER 9

Dear father,

According to the promise I made before I left home, it becomes my painful duty to announce to you that I am sick. I do not know how it came about but it is so. I, one night ate some syrup that was not very good, and it did not agree with me. My bowels were very much relaxed the next morning. I have been sick alternately, for 8 or 10 days. I do not think that I am in any danger. I think I will be able for duty in 4 or 5 days.

Our regiment was ordered off from here yesterday. They left 17 men belonging to our company at the old camp.

Father, you never saw the like of sick men in your life. We have about 200 sick now at one place. I am in my old tent and the rest gone the first time I have ever been left on the account of sickness yet. And I hope it will be the last time. For I had rather be sick any where else than in camp.

Father, I have gotten one letter only since I left home from you, and I reckon I would not have gotten that one had Mr. Chaney not brought it. I have recieved one from Ma, one from sister Elizabeth, and one from brother Thomas. I have also received some from my Talbot friends. I want you all to write to me oftener than you do.

Father, tell brother R.S. and brother Joseph Williams, I think they ought to write to me.

I have written about 12 or 14 letters to the family and friends since I left home, and I think it is time I was getting some.

Father, I am so much fatigued that I cannot write anymore. I am very weak and can't write as much as I want to.

Father, give my love to all the family and friends who many enquire about me.

Your loving son,

H.C. Kendrick

LETTER 9 REPLY

Dear H.C.,

My mother would often leave me treats on the kitchen table: a candy bar, a cupcake, or maybe super sweet maple syrup to go with the pancakes she made me before she began running errands. Looking back now, maybe that was the "*kiss*" I thought I never received.

It was good being the only child. I was spoiled at times for certain. Without a sibling, I never had to share anything that my parents gave me. But that also meant I had no one to help me with the chores.

Next to my treat, my mother typically left a note reminding me of what needed to be done that day, whether that was polishing the floor or emptying all the home's trashcans.

Then again, perhaps you are not the one to whom I should complain about chores.

Your father and the slaves, along with the women in those days, had to plow the corn, hoe the field, milk the cows, prepare the meals, clean the home, and so on.

You and your siblings were then expected to do the same.

Prior to joining the war effort, you certainly had more to do at home than I did.

Then again, you had help. You had people around you.

I am sure that you can sense my conflict.

I understand your loneliness.

You didn't directly say you were lonely, but you certainly implied it through that last letter when you implored your father to write.

For the first time in your life, you were away from home for an extended period. You were still leaning on your family for support, but only through words scribed on paper. You must have missed their presence, their voices, their cadences, and even their worst habits that once drove you nuts.

Yes, I understand your loneliness because, as an only child, I often felt like I was the sole resident of an island.

Most of my neighborhood friends had siblings and, as kids will do, we'd sometimes get into arguments. When it escalated, one of their siblings would often join in on their side. Older brothers would threaten to kick my butt. Sometimes, older sisters would too. Younger siblings would toss a barrage of insults at me, defeating me in an oral battle through sheer numbers.

I'd then go home, dejected, and wonder how cool it would be if I had an older brother who had my back.

Life as an only child can be sweet. But life as an only child can also be lonely.

I do not envy the illness you were battling when you wrote that letter.

But I do envy your large family you had for support.

I wonder if I could have leaned on siblings with my secret, had I had any.

You were luckier than you know.

Then again, I also never had to experience the loss that your family experienced. Besides your mother, you lost a brother.

I read in our family history that your brother Joseph died in 1854, at just 9 years old. Family history recalled him as full of fun and laughter and the athletic type who was always willing to perform stunts.

Then one evening, the family heard a gurgling moaning sound and they found him lying in a pool of blood. He'd burst a blood vessel. He was buried next to your mother.

I guess loneliness and sadness are relative to what we know.

Your loving nephew,

Ben

LETTER 10

Camp near Centerville, Va.

November 10th, 1861

Dear father and mother,
I have received my clothing last night, was glad to get them.
You don't have any idea how much relieved I was when I got
them. I am under so many obligations to you for sending to
me some clothing. They came in the proper time. I was just
about out of clothes when they came, but would have not been
out, if I had not gotten a letter from you stating that you
had sent me some clothing, I kept waiting for them until I got
almost without any at all.

Ma. tell sister Sallie, that I am under ten thousand of obli-
gations to her for sending me that bottle of good wine. But tell
her, that it did not last me more than 30 minutes. The boys of
my mess all loved it so well, that they could not refrain from
asking me for it, I could not refuse them but told them to help
them-selves. So they took me at my word.

Ma. may the Lord bless you, may he give to you comfort
and peace as long as you live and after death comes may he
still uphold you and give you a full and free acceptance in the
heavenly kingdom.

Ma. and Pa. please accept my earnest and undissembling
thanks to you. You must not think of me feign. I was glad to
hear from brother B.C.K. Tell him I will write to him before
long.

I don't know that I have any thing of very striking interest
to write to you at present. The war here is played out for the
present. I don't think we will have any fighting at this place
this winter.

I was talking with Gen. Jones[1], (our brigadeer Gen.) the
other day and he said that he did not think there would be

---

1 This is Samuel Jones, who was appointed a brigadier general on July 21,

much more fighting. He said he did not think there would be any fight here at all. Although we have gotten the news here that the enemy were advancing.

Father, we just lying here in camps doing nothing. We are tired lying in camps. We can't get any thing to do. I think I will forget how to do any thing in three years.

This leaves me in good health. You must write soon as you get this.

Your loving son,

H. C. Kendrick

P.S. My clothes fit me as well as if I had been there to try them on. Give my love to all of the family and friends of that neighborhood.

Yours,

H.C.K.

1861, and who served under Gen. P.G.T. Beauregard. He was later promoted to major general on March 10, 1862. Surrendered in Tallahassee, Florida on May 10, 1865. After the war he served as president to the Maryland Agricultural College, from 1873 to 1875. He died in Bedford Springs, Pennsylvania on July 31, 1887, age 67.

LETTER 10 REPLY

Dear H.C.

Since the war was played out for the present when you wrote that letter, perhaps now is the time to detail that horrific day in my childhood.

I have delayed telling you about it until I was ready and until the time was right. I felt selfish discussing my bad fortune in reply to letters from the warfront. Your situation was more dire than mine.

So, here goes ...

I believe I was 6 or 7 years old, based on the school I was attending at the time and the fact that I was allowed to ride my bike around the neighborhood on my own, as all kids of that age were allowed to do back then. We had more trust in society back then, more so than people do today, a trust that was broken on this day.

It also had to be sometime between Spring and Fall, because I recall leaves still being on the trees, and because I was wearing shorts..

My best friend suggested that we trek around the neighborhood on our bikes to look for other kids with whom to play.

We made it about a block when my friend stopped at a particular house. A boy, around our age, was sitting in front of a house.

My friend introduced him as Duane Crockett. The name immediately struck me as odd. But, even odder, was that Duane said he'd lived in the neighborhood for a while. How can that be, I wondered, when I had never seen him before?

But I was so young. I wasn't going to question anything. I was just happy we had another kid with whom to play.

Duane invited us inside the house. I think he wanted to get a drink of water or something. The details escape me all these years later. But I will never forget the old lady who was inside. She was sitting in a rocking chair and just rocking back and forth, staring ahead like she was deaf and blind and had no idea we were in the room. But I don't think she was either. I think she was just out of it for whatever reason.

It was so creepy that I cheered inside my head when Duane re-emerged from wherever he'd gone and suggested we go back outside to play. It was so hot, I recall, that Duane's driveway asphalt had softened, and my kickstand had pushed into it.

My friend and I then left and rode around the neighborhood on our bikes for a bit and each went home for dinner.

Two weeks later, I was walking around the neighborhood on my own when I again saw Duane. He was again just hanging out alone, on the sidewalk near his house. He waved me over and asked if I wanted to play, explaining that he had a whole basement full of toys.

That sounded pretty good to me. I didn't have a lot of toys.

Rather than taking me inside his house, Duane led me across the street to another house, from where a man was watching us from the second-story window. He hung out the window up to his chest and told us to go through the back door if we wanted to play with the toys.

Duane led me into the basement. It was unfinished. No carpeting, no furniture, nothing. It had just a concrete floor and cinderblock walls. But there were certainly lots of toys against one of those walls. I rushed over to check out the variety but, before I could dig in, the strange man entered the basement.

I remember initially wondering if the man was my cousin's husband. He looked just like him. Blonde hair, medium build, around 5'10. But I quickly realized this was not the face of a friendly family member.

That man stood in a way that he blocked the entrance and stared at me without the slightest look of joy. I had a feeling something was wrong. I was absolutely terrified.

I stared at the strange man for what felt like hours but was likely seconds.

He then addressed me. He never raised his voice or spoke aggressively, yet he seemed menacing.

"You're welcome to play with those toys," he told me, "But big boys don't play with toys. Only little girls do."

"Am I a girl," he asked, "or a boy?"

I didn't reply. I just stood, frozen.

He then told me that, "I could do whatever I wanted when at his house. I could even pee on the floor," he said. "Ain't that right Duane," he continued, "go ahead, show your friend that we can pee on the floor."

And Duane did.

When I didn't pee on the floor too, the man pulled out a pocketknife.

He again asked if I was a girl and, still without raising his voice, said that "he could cut off my penis and make me a girl if I wanted to play with those toys."

A switch went off in my head at that moment that has never been flipped back the other way. At that moment, I entered another world, a scary and confusing world that no child should ever know exists. A grown man was threatening to cut off my penis if I played with toys instead of peeing on the floor.

So, I peed on the floor.

The moment I finished, he matter-of-factly said to let him suck on it.

I stood there, frozen as he did.

He then took his out and told me to do the same to his or he would turn me into a little girl.

That moment changed my entire life.

Before I left, confused, the strange man made one more threat: If I ever spoke of what happened to anyone, he would cut off my penis and then murder my parents.

From that moment on, my view of the world was different.

I was never the same again.

Yours,

Ben

LETTER 11

Dear father,

I again seat my-self to write to you. You may think strange of me for writing so soon after having writen. The reason I seat my-self to write to you is, that you asked me to tell you all that I have to do; and all I have not to do.

In the first place, I will tell you what I have to. That is this: I have to drill battalion drill once a day that is generally, though I have not drilled in a week, because we have had no drill in that space of time. There is one more duty I have to do that is, to go out on dress parade. It comes late in the evening, about half an hour by sun. You, I guess, have not much idea of that.

Now I will tell you, to give you an idea of it. The regiment goes out and forms a line on some level place in an old field, we stand there until we are commanded by our captains several-ly, to order arms. We order arms, then the command is given by the captains, separately parade rest, we then throw our right feet in the rear of our left, and stand in that position un-til the band of music plays up and down the line after which, the adjutant[1] – whos place is at the right of the regiment, steps 6 paces from the regiment and gives the command. Attention battalion – shoulder arms, after which, he walks down the line to the center of the Regt. at which place, he turns to the right and walks about ten paces from the Regt. Then turns about and gives the command present arms. Then turns about and salutes the Col. and tells him the parade is formed. The Col. returns the salute and the adjutant walks to the left of the Col. then the Col. draws his sword and carries the battalion

---

1   Adjutant refers to a military officer who acts as an administrative assistant to a senior officer.

through all the manual of arms he thinks proper and sheathes his sword then the adjutant walks within ten paces of the battalion and gives the command first sergeants, to the front, and center-march. And orders them to give a report of their men. They give a report then he gives the command to the sergeants Outward face, to your post - march then he abouts and reports to the Col. Then the parade is dismissed.

Father, I have been a long time telling you about it, but it is as short as the old saying is a rusted grubworm. We are about one half an hour doing it all.

Now father you perceive that I do not have much to do. Well I will now tell you what I do not have to do. I do not have to drill company drill, don't have to stand guard, to throw up breast works, do not cut wood, don't hall wood, make bridges, work the road, clean up camps, nor do any thing else. In fact I am released from all hard-ships pertaining to a soldier's life. Father, I have a very easy time indeed.

Now you may think it strange that I am released from all thes duties. I simply guard the colors when we get into a fight. I will then be in great danger, because as a matter of course, the enemy will try to shoot the colors down. Of course I will be in great danger.

Father, write to me as soon as you can.

O yes, Samuel Fuller got a letter from Alpheus Fuller stating that brother Thomas was first Corporal. I was glad to hear of that. Write to him and tell him I say go it, do his best for his country, I wish I was with him.

I have seen Cousin Daniel Kendrick. I did not see B. &S. They were at the hospital sick. They are in the 15th Ala. Regiment. In Col. Canty's[2] care. Dan looked natural.

---

2   James Cantey, helped form the 15th Alabama Infantry Regiment in 1861, they elected him their colonel. He was engaged throughout many battles from Alabama, Virginia, Tennessee, Georgia, and finally North Carolina where he surrendered. A lawyer, and former South Carolina state legislator, and slave owner. After the Civil War he returned home to his plantation, and died ten years later, June 30, 1874, age 55.

I also have seen Dr. Kendrick, but do not know where he is now, nor do I know his regiment. I have seen Jos. Connel, he is in the 2ᴰ. Regt. That Regt. is a mile from ours.

Father, we have plenty of bed clothing. I will tell you the boys that compose my mess: Samuel Fuller, William Brooks, Dr. Childs, Erasmus Persons, Cole Buchanan, H.C. Kendrick. We all have about 24 blankets, and 2 coverlets, so we keep warm at night. We have a very large tent, that we have gotten since we came out here.

Well Pa. you may tell the girls that they had better not worry until the soldiers get back there. Tell them they are just as good cooks as they ever saw in their lives.

Ma, I expect I can make as good biscuits as you can. I expect I can beat you if you will give me the same means that you have. I can beat any body in the Regiment making biscuits. When I get home I will try to beat you making biscuits Ma.

I must close for this time, give my love to all.

Your son,

H. C. Kendrick

LETTER 11 REPLY

Dear H.C.,

During my 17th summer, another teenager and I were hired to dig the area where a foundation would go for a home located in the Virginia woods. An old man dropped us off at the spot in his truck, handed us shovels and picks and a water keg, and said he'd see us in eight hours.

We had to be half a mile down a dirt road and so far from civilization that we could hear another vehicle coming from miles away.

That was some hard work. It was a dull and miserable job. The ground was more rock than dirt, making it difficult to break up. And we were making very little money. Making it even worse was that our boss, who made more money than us, spent the day at the bar while we worked.

One day, I'd estimate four hours into our work, we gave up and plopped on our butts for the next few hours until we heard his truck approaching. We then leapt to our feet and pretended like we'd been working the entire time.

As we climbed into his truck, the old man asked for how many hours he should pay us because we obviously did not work the full day.

We feigned shock. What does he mean, we shot back, we'd only taken a short break for lunch.

With a laugh, he climbed into the truck and told us that the next time we want to get away with laziness, we should brush the dirt off our butts. There was enough caked on, he said, that it was obvious we'd sat for a long time.

I tell you that story to illustrate what true laziness looks like.

You seemed determined to let your father know that you were indeed a hard worker, despite being allowed to skip some chores due to your status as color guard.

H.C., no one would have ever thought anything negative about a color guard. No one doubted that position made you the bravest on the battlefield. You were defenseless as you carried the flag representing your cause.

I understand why the Confederacy would have wanted you to serve as color guard. You were the type of man they want to be a symbol of the Confederacy – young, handsome, educated and from an upstanding family.

But I do not understand why you were willing to take on that job.

When a lamb was sacrificed to the gods, they always chose the fattest and the prettiest because that is what the gods deserved.

I am not calling you fat. Ha. But you are the sacrificial lamb.

Did you take that position because you so believed in the cause? Or did you take it to prove your bravery? Or, perhaps, did you feel like you had no choice once it was offered.

I have to think your father's heart sank when he read this letter. He was always against this war. He preferred to remain in the Union. And now, his son was representing the Confederacy. His son was the face of the cause during battle and was the primary target for the other side.

My heart sank when I read your letter.

Little did you know when you accepted that position and wrote that letter that the decision to serve as color guard is why you did not live to have a wife, children, a career, and so on. That decision doomed you.

In the same way, I think of that day I agreed to go into that stranger's home to play with some toys. How would my life have differed if I had not?

Your nephew,

Ben

P.S. I cannot believe you told your mother that your biscuits were better than hers. You were indeed brave. Ha.

P.S. H.C., well I have to confess, after all my reading and your talking about biscuits, I took up "The Biscuit Challenge"! I am a pretty fair cook, mind you! I researched first the ingredients, and what makes the best biscuit. I also prefer organic ingredients, so I made sure I could obtain them. I even went into several antique stores, you guessed it, in old Va., in search of a biscuit cutter. Yep, found it, perfect size in diameter with a handle.

Well, over the course of a few weeks, and several biscuit batches from scratch later - flour all over the kitchen counter, many times, and on my shirt, jeans, and on the floor, many times - my sweetheart and I had some biscuits! Fresh, fluffy, and hot out of the oven. We drowned them in melted butter and enjoyed! Like you said, *"fat as a pig in a pen......."*

LETTER 12

Camp near Centerville Va.

November 15th, 1861

Dear sisters,

I am now just off picket. When I went there, I found a large booth in which, I threw my bundle of bed clothing. Then being free from all disturbances, I sat down under my booth and after having been at ease for some time I was soon inwrapt by a deep and solemn meditation.

I was struck with the importance of the post which we held. Then the most dangerous of all others. I felt under strong responsibilities knowing that the very destination of our country depended upon the care we took in guarding that line. Then arose the great pleasure which I used to enjoy at home with my dear beloved relatives and friends. These thoughts struck me with force.

Sisters I even thought of my old desk by which, I have often seated my-self for my improvement. That thought met my tallent precisely. But sis, the most important of all, and the part that afforded me the most pleasure of all, was this: that after a while, if we faint not in the end, a bright and glorious victory will be ours. Sisters I think we are bound to have it. I see nothing to prevent. How can it be other wise? Is it possible for a low, a degraded Set of Northern people to be victorious over a noble and respectable squad of Southerners? Men that are fighting through a pure motive? Vindicating the rights of the South? No, I say it is not.

Well sisters I have suffered a great deal with cold for the last 4 days. The weather is getting very cold. The wind has been blowing without intermission for 4 or 5 days, and very cold too. It is about as much as I can do, to stay away from the fire long enough to write a short letter.

We will, I guess, go into winter quarters before long. But what kind of winter quarters do you guess they will be? Why I will tell you. We will go into such as we have been into all the time. That is the kind we will go into. The boys in my mess, intend to fix up for the winter. We intend to put up a kind of house to keep us from the wind. I think we will fix up pretty well.

Now sisters, don't think me dissatisfied at all. For I think I am as well satisfied as any body could be in an engagement of this kind. But I was simply giving you the description of my situation.

Sisters we took 32 prisoners day before yesterday, and took 5, 4-horse waggons, and 100 bushels of corn. So there was a pretty good lick for us as corn is scarce. We have 6 other prisoners at Centerville now.

Sisters E.K., Sallie Williams, Mary Kendrick, Ann Kendrick, I will send you ten dollars for you 4 to all share alike in it. I do it for your kindness to me. You will then enclosed.

I am getting very cold. I will close for the present.

My health is good, give my love to all the family and friends and more especially the girls of that neighborhood.

I remain your affectionate brother,

H. C. Kendrick.

P.S. you will please send me my Bullions' Lattin grammer and reader[1], and an English grammer.

Your brother
H.C.K.

---

1   *Bullions' Latin Grammar* by Rev. Peter Bullions, D.D., Professor of Languages in the Albany Academy, and author of the Series of Grammer, Greek, Latin, and English. Bullions was born in Perthshire, Scotland, December 1791, and died in Troy, Vermont, USA in February 1864, age 72. Two years after his death, Asahel C. Kendrick, (possibly a relative to the author) and American Grammarian, revised his *Principles of Greek Grammar*, published 1866.

LETTER 12 REPLY

Dear H.C.,

"My health is good, give my love to all the family and friends and more especially the girls of that neighborhood."

Especially the girls … that reminds of something my Uncle Ben might have said.

Perhaps my coolest relative was my Uncle Ben, also Benjamin Burks Kendrick. He was from New York and walked around with that New York swagger that let you know he was always the coolest guy in the room just because he was from the coolest city in the United States.

I will never forget the time he visited and brought me a leather jacket. I was probably 5 or 6 and it was without a doubt the coolest present I had ever received. I wanted to wear it everywhere and all the time, even if it was 100 degrees.

He also had a real disdain for the Southern culture. He always spoke poorly of that region solely because of the way they treated Black men and women. He looked down on Arlington for that reason too. We were more progressive than the deep South, but we still had a segregated society.

I stayed in New York with him several times. He had the sweetest wife, Elsie Lowe. She always greeted me with a sincere hug.

I was probably 5 the first time that I visited him in New York. I travelled there on a train, by myself. My mother took me to Union Station and onto the train heading for New York and asked the woman sitting next to me if she would look after me until my uncle got me. It was a giant adventure. I was on a train for the first time in my life, staring out the window for the entire three- or four-hour trip, watching the world zoom past.

Uncle Ben was waiting for me as I stepped off the train into Penn Station.

He took me directly to a café located in the corner of a cavernous room inside the station. My uncle got himself a coffee and me a Coke, and then chatted with the café's Black employee for a few minutes, introducing me as his favorite nephew since we shared a name, and asking the employee about his family. It was obvious from the conversation that they knew one another well.

As we left the café, he waved to the employee and then said to me in a very matter-of-fact voice, "Up here, Black people are treated as equals."

I have written these letters as though you are aware of all that is going on in modern society. And I believe you do.

So, I believe that you have learned that a Black man has been president, a Black man and woman have been Supreme Court justices, and Black people have proven that they are equals in every way. They have proven that skin color does not dictate ability.

I am torn on what to think about my ancestors enslaving others.

On the one hand, I agree with the argument that we should not judge those from past generations on the morals of today.

On the other hand, it is hard to understand how it was ever thought to be OK.   .

On one hand, though your enslaved totaled only five as compared to dozens at other properties, five still seems too many.

On the other hand, your family performed the same work as they did, whether in the home or the field.

On one hand, you and your family thought it was OK to own another human being.

On the other hand, by all family accounts, your family treated all those they enslaved humanely.

For instance, there was the enslaved woman your family learned was being beaten by her plantation owner and was to be forced to carry children against her will. So, they purchased her and treated her like your family.

But the most famous family story is of Joe, the enslaved man whom your grandfather found near his new Georgia home as he was clearing the woods. Joe was deaf and mute and had apparently been living in a camp that he built. He had been doing so for quite a while, maybe years. He threw himself at your grandfather's feet. Your family fed him, provided him with water and gave him clothes. When public officials learned of him and said he had to be sold, your grandfather purchased him to ensure Joe a better life, built him a home of his own on the plantation, and worked him reasonable hours. He stayed with your family until his death and was loved.

On the one hand, I commend your family for his treatment.

On the other hand, couldn't they have just left him at his camp in the woods?

Your family believed in God and studied the Bible. So, you all must have been aware of the Golden Rule: Do unto others as you would have done unto you.

Then again, some who enslaved the Black men, women, and children did not believe they were men, women, and children. Some believed they were animals who needed the white man to civilize them. At least, that is how it appears the South rationalized enslaving them. I wonder if they all believed that to be true.

The Southern states relied on slavery and surely the leaders knew the economy would collapse without them. So, how did they get the everyday people to support enslaving others? By teaching them that they were lesser and needed to be conquered. That is how governments have been convincing men and women to go to war against an enemy since the beginning of time.

The Nazis were taught the Jews were evil, so participated in genocide.

The United States was taught that Communists were evil so that our people would support a flurry of armed conflicts against them.

Muslims in the Middle East were taught that Americans were evil in order to radicalize them as terrorists, and, some Americans were taught that the Muslims in the Middle East were evil in order to radicalize them as terrorists.

And you, H.C., and those you fought beside had been taught that the Yankees were evil in order to convince you to fight them without guilt. I wonder, if you took the time to speak with the *"degraded set of Northern people"* and learned that they are just like you, would you still have wanted to kill them?

Once again, please do not think I am exonerating the northern powers-that-be. They too sold their people a bill of goods to get them to fight that war. The Union needed the Confederate states, or their economy would have tanked. The war has historically often been framed as one that was only about ending slavery. But if it were about slavery, the United States would have sought to abolish it years before. They waited until the South's growing prosperity threatened the wealthy Northerners.

The economy is run by the three P's – Providers, Producers and Parasites or (pimps). *I was unable to find a more refined word that started with P- you see, it's about rhythm.*

Providers are those who create the raw goods, like cotton. The South was the Provider of the economy in your time.

Producers are those who turn those raw goods into needed items. The North had the factories. They were the Producers.

The North needed the South, but the South did not need the North. When the Civil War began, the South was getting into the factory business and likely would have succeeded if left to be on their own. The North did not care about slaves. They cared about keeping the South under their control so that they had goods to produce. The issue of slavery was just a way to convince men of the needs to go to war. They might not have done so if told they had to fight so that the rich Northern factory owners could get richer.

As for the third P – Parasites or (pimps), they are those who provide no actual services yet find a way to not only leach off others, but also direct them to do their bidding. They are the ones who convince us it is in our best interest to go to war and enslave others for the benefit of their bottom line.

They are the ones who convince us to commit atrocities against men, women and even children.

Your loving nephew,

Ben.

LETTER 13

Dear father,

Yours of the 20th ult.[1] came to hand last night. I was exceedingly glad to hear from you. You stated in your letter that you had not received a letter from me since the 27th of September. If I haven't written a half dozen since that time, I haven't written any at all. So I guess there has been some defect in the postmasters. They have not attended to their business.

The letter that I got last night from you and Ma was, except the letters that came in those large boxes which came for the company, the only one I have gotten since the 28th of Sept. You, also stated in your letter, that Dr. Mains said we were naked, we were not entirely so, but a good many were in that fix. I was not so bad off as that my-self. I have received the clothing you sent by Henry Bryan, and have gotten some that were sent by Mr. Miller. So I have plenty of clothes now. I have enough to do me until next Spring. I am doing exceedingly well at the present.

You said something about the money I sent for. I did borrow ten dollars from one of the boys sure enough just as you said you would do. I made out very well. I have drawn money since that time, and paid back the money I borrowed. I am doing very well in the money sensation. You need not send me any money now. We will draw again next January, then I will see if I can't send you some. I, if I am not deluded, can send you 20 or 25 dollars at that time. I sent $10 by Henry Bryan to Ma. and sisters Eliz., Mary Kendrick, and Sallie Williams.

---

1   ult. – in American English typically means ultimo, ultimate, ultimately.

I had that much much more than I wanted and consequently would not keep it.

We are well fixed up now, considering the means which we have with which to fix that is our mess. We have put up a scaffold for lying on about 1 foot above the ground. We have plenty of covering at night. I sleep very warm these cold nights.

Ma. you wrote me word that you sent me 2 boxes, in which was the very kind of provision I wanted. I have not gotten them yet though William Brooks has gone to the Junction to-day to look for them. Perhaps he will find them.

Ma. there seemed to have been some little contention about the march that was taken by our boys from Winchester to Piedmont. You wanted me to settle the contention so I will. I was not in the company at that time. I was at Winchester at the time.

Pa let me tell you not to be uneasy about me, for I am getting along better than I or you, ever expected that I would get along. I have plenty to eat and but little to do. I never have any thing to do at all that is hard, not even to stand guard. I am entirely released from all duty. So, you may know that I have an easy time.

I must close for the present. Give my love to all the family and friends.

I remain your loving son,

H. C. Kendrick

LETTER 13 REPLY

Dear H.C.,

My parents were far from poor, but they were also far from wealthy.

I had friends with wealthy parents who drove around these brand-new American made cars while my parents owned cheap cars, some American and some foreign.

The same went for my bicycle. I had friends who always pedaled around on shiny bikes, whereas mine was one of the cheapest made. It didn't have brakes, so my feet had to do that job, and the chain was always falling off.

I'd complain, but my father would counter that I could buy my own. Meanwhile, he said, I had to take care of the upkeep on my cheap bike.

He wasn't trying to be mean. He wanted to instill me with independence.

I can tell your father did the same with you.

You were not asking him to send you more than you absolutely needed, and you sent him whatever money you did not require.

My earliest jobs were paper routes.

I first delivered the *Northern Virginia Sun*. I was 11, an age that is easy to remember because I took the job shortly after President John F. Kennedy was assassinated.

It was a short route along Ridge Road. I maybe had a few dozen customers. But most of those customers were important men and woman who worked in high-ranking positions at the Pentagon, including David Shoup, the commandant of the Marine Corps. I'd estimate I made a whopping $10 a month.

I next moved on to the *Washington Star*, which was the second biggest newspaper in that area at the time but is no longer in business today. I got a dollar per month per delivery, which equaled three cents a newspaper per day. I can't recall how many newspapers I delivered, but I know I made more than I did at the *Sun*.

From there, I took a job selling subscriptions for the *Washington Star*.

A man named Mr. Sowers loaded three or four of us into the back of his Pontiac Bonneville and drove us block to block to knock on doors. We worked the neighborhoods of Alexandria, Arlington, and a small portion of the District of Columbia.

We had to memorize the same sales pitch. Everyone was to be referred to as ma'am or sir and each subscription came with a 90-day money back guarantee.

I still recall my reaction to the first paycheck. Where is all my money, I demanded to know. The government took it, Mr. Sowers shot back. It is called taxes, he explained with a laugh.

The job had perks. The newspaper once gave all of our crew tickets to watch a college football game between Penn State and Navy at RFK Stadium in Washington D.C.

It also taught me humility. I saw my first color TV while pitching subscriptions. I was so mesmerized that I forgot my pitch as I stared at it and promised that I would one day own one.

I now own several big screens, as they are called now, and appreciate each because I earned them myself.

That's how I was raised.

So were you.

You were a fine young man, H.C.

I remain your loving nephew,

Ben

P.S. T.V. stands for television, it is kind of like an ambrotype photograph, but a little bit more complex. The subject is captured with movement and sound to be viewed by an audience.

LETTER 14

Head Quarters, Smith's Division[1],

Camp near Centerville,

Dec. 1st, 1861

Dear brother,

I received your letter of the 10th ult. and was very glad to know, that you take interest enough in your own improvement to undertake to write. I think you did extremely well for one of your age.

Binnie, you must forgive me, for not having written before now to you. Binnie, I don't feel well enough to write this evening, notwithstanding, I feel like as it is one of my dear brothers, I must write.

I wrote to cousin Mollie Trussell a few days ago stating, that I was about well of the mumps; but since that time, I have taken the fever which has gone rather hard with me. I have gotten very weak from the effects of it. But we have one advantage of which, you are not aware; and that is this: we have a very good chimney attached to our tent and a good fire place which I find to be very advantageous to us. I keep in my tent very closely. We have very cold and unpleasant weather here now. It is windy all the time.

But we don't have any thing scarcely to do, but cook, eat, and sleep. The Col. doesn't put any guards out at all. I expect we will go into winter quarters before long.

Now Binnie, my shoulders hurt me so badly, I must close. You must not forget to write to me again. You must write to me every chance you have.

---

1   Led by General William Smith, also known as "Extra Billy" for establishing extra mail routes from Washington, D.C. to the Carolinas to Georgia in 1831. Entering the war unexpectedly on June 1, 1861, at the battle of Fairfax Court House. He was 64 at the time and former Governor of Virginia. At the time of the Battle of Gettysburg he was Virginia Governor-Elect, at 65, he would be the oldest general to serve in the Battle of Gettysburg. Received honorary promotion to Major General and remained in Warrenton, Virginia, where he continued public service to age 82, and died at age 89.

Give my love to all the family.

I remain your loving brother,

H. C. Kendrick

LETTER 14 REPLY

Dear H.C.,

Maybe a year after I was assaulted, we moved a few blocks away.

It wasn't far from that man's house, but it was far enough. Prior to that move, I had to pass it while on my way to school. I would always walk on the other side of the street and, if no one was around to question why I was acting strange, I would sprint until the house was in the distance.

What seemed strange, though, is that I never saw any signs that anyone lived there. It looked empty.

Nor did I ever see Duane Crockett at the house where he supposedly lived. It was like all that I experienced was a nightmare that never really happened.

And, for a while, I thought it was.

Then, I saw Duane again.

The summer after my assault, shortly before we moved, I was sent to Day Camp for part of the summer. Each day centered around some sort of day trip, either to the museum, or a park, or a pool.

On one occasion, they gathered all the kids onto a bus and took us to a golf course driving range on Mount Vernon Avenue alongside Four Mile Run. It was this giant field filled with golf balls. We were each given a basket and told to collect as many balls as we could.

You wrote of having little to do. Well, this might be the peak of having little to do. The camp must have been all out of ideas.

But it was fun for us. It was like a giant Easter Egg hunt.

In retrospect, we were being used as free labor. I wonder if the camp received a kickback from the golf course for taking us there to do their work.

We weren't the only camp there that day. There was at least one more and Duane was among the campers. We locked eyes, but he quickly averted his as though he never saw me. But I ran to him as fast as I could and tapped him on the shoulder.

He spun around, surprised, and scared.

We both froze. I felt weak, as though I was the one with mumps.

But I had to ask. "Have you seen that man? That man, have you seen him?"

Duane didn't reply. He just stared and blinked like his eyes were the only part of his body not frozen.

"Ok, I'll see you later," I finally said after what could have been a few seconds or minutes, and I ran off.

I never saw Duane again.

And it wasn't until recently, as I went through this exercise of writing these letters, that I began to think about him in depth.

Duane was in the basement with me the entire time.

He watched as I was assaulted. I have always wondered what happened to Duane.

I remain your loving nephew,

Ben

LETTER 15

Camp near Centerville,

Dec. 29th, 1861

Dear father,
Just having returned off picket, I feel like writing. We had a very good time out there. When we got there, we went out on the out line; about 1 mile from the camp, [that's]¹ the camp; that we [call] reserve camp. When [we] got there the weather was cold. The orders [were that] we should have no [fires] the different posts; but it was so cold, we had fire any how. As I haven't time to give you a full detail of our trip, I will not make the attempt. Our Capt. is going to start to Ga. tomorrow morning, for which reason, I write this evening.

Father, I tell you, I am exceedingly sorry that we have to lose our Capt.², for he suits us better than any one else could. He has had bad health for 2 or 3 months, and is not able to fill the place of [a soldier.] I am almost as [sad] to separate from [him,] as I was to leave [home] enough.

Father, [we] are going into winter [quarters,] and I wish you and ma. to send me some lard, butter, sausage, and several other little things; you know what I need better than I do.

---

1   This letter in The Collection has a small piece cut out from the side of the letter; thereby text was lost. However, portions of some of the words were discernible. Author has made assumptions to missing text. We also noted where the piece was cut out, H.C. began to write "I am....". We can only assume, he may have disclosed where the Regiment was, and intelligence removed the information by cutting the letter.

2   Ninth Georgia Infantry, Company E, Talbot Guards, Captain was P.A.S. Morris. He resigned January 1862.

I haven't the time to write any more. Give my love to all the family.

I will write again soon.

Your loving son,

H. C. Kendrick

LETTER 15 REPLY

Dear H.C.,

I have learned so much about your father and your relationship with him that perhaps now is a good time to tell you about my father and that side of my family.

The Buckleys came to the United States from Ireland and eventually settled in California during the Gold Rush. They were real life 49ers.

They never did find enough gold to rise from rags to riches, so they became boilermakers and owned a company in San Francisco.

From what I understand, when my grandfather was in his 20s, he was put on a ship to Alaska to build a boiler for the Del Monte Foods, Inc.[1] who made their fortune in food production and distribution. He was injured in some way while on that ship, treated with morphine, and was an addict from that point on.

Somehow, he convinced my grandmother to marry him anyway, even after he added alcoholism to his drug addiction.

A devout Catholic, my grandmother worried a divorce would land her in hell and believed that she could pray my grandfather's addictions away. But she was not naïve enough to believe that the home was stable enough for a child.

So, when my father was a kid, he was sent to live with relatives in Oakland.

Then came the Second World War.

Luckily for my father, the battles were over by the time he joined. So, he was shipped off to England as part of the effort to rebuild that European nation that had suffered great trauma from the Nazi bombings.

---

1   The Del Monte Foods Inc. was named after the luxury hotel in Monterey, California.

He worked primarily as a typist in one of the Army offices and had the opportunity to explore France and Germany during extended leaves. He said he saw a lot of devastation but also drank a lot of alcohol. He even met one of the Rothschild family, who made their fortune in banking, finance, mining, and a slew of other ventures. It is safe to say that my father's experiences in the military were much different from yours.

When his time in the military was up, he had no desire to return to California, so he headed to the Arlington County-Washington D.C. area to use the G.I. Bill to attend Georgetown University's School of Foreign Service with a goal of one day working in the State Department.

That was his dream, he told me. He wanted to make a career out of serving his country.

Unfortunately, he was never given the chance.

He was working a clerical job for the U.S. Government while still in school when he was fired without any chance of ever being hired back.

They didn't want his kind.

His kind was a homosexual.

My dad was gay.

So was my mother.

I know that is a lot to digest, so I will explain more later.

Your loving nephew,

Ben

LETTER 16

Camp Sam Jones[1]

Feb. 2nd, 1862

Dear brother & sister,

I received your very kind, interesting, and highly esteemed letter yesterday. It was well and carefully perused. You have no idea how much consolation it affords me to hear from home. You cannot write to me too often, you cannot make it too common a thing to be not negligently read by me.

Dear brother, I would like to be able to give you some idea of the proceedings of the war; but they are inscrutable, they elude my mental grasp, lead them into perfect obscurity, and almost reduces them to incomprehensibility.

You stated in your letter, that sister E had not fully decided whether she would go to school or not. Tell her for me, that I think she had better go to school every day she has the opportunity; for there is nothing so valuable as the accomplishment of a good education. Consequently, would advise her to avail her-self of the present.

You said that you had not gotten the little money, that I sent home. I would like you [to] go to him and demand it.

The snow lies 4 inches deep on the ground now; and it is still falling in great haste. I think it by night, will be 6 or 8 inches deep.

You said, that Ma., had no chance to safely send me a box of provision, well, I can tell you a good chance to send it to me: Mr. H. Peed is at home, you can send it by him.

---

1   Camp Sam Jones probably was near Centreville, Virginia. Samuel Jones, former graduate of West Point, and served in the US Army upon his resignation in 1861 to become a brigadier general for the Confederate Army. Promoted to Major General in 1862. Commanded many major Departments of the War, including Western Virginia, Tennessee, Florida, and Georgia, until his surrender in Tallahassee, Florida in 1865. He later served as a College President and died in 1887, age 67.

Brother, you said you wanted to send me some little things; for which, I will be very thankful to you. Having been raised by a good mother, and kind sisters, by whose kindness I have gotten such things, and at whose hands I have been comforted, such things as those will be very palitable.

Now, I will give you a dol of the prices of different things here for sale.

pork, 12 1/2 cts. per pound, meal 100 per bushel, flour $6 per bbl., chickens grown, are worth 50 cts, turkeys $1,50 cts, cooked $2,00, and beef, it is unnecessary for me to say any thing about it; for I have eaten it until I am almost ashamed to meet a cow in the road; their heads and horns are lying upon these old hills like light wood knots north of your house.

I have had good health for the last month. My health is good now. I must close.

Give my love to all the family.

Write soon, your affectionate brother,
H. C. Kendrick

LETTER 16 REPLY

Dear H.C.,

I apologize for ending my last letter so abruptly and not writing more about the revelation that my parents were both gay.

It's a hard topic for me to discuss and not because I am ashamed of them. There is ZERO shame in being gay. It is how they were born, and I am proud that they tried to live honest lives before the government forced them to retreat to the closet.

Still, it is hard to discuss because I was kept in the dark for so long.

My mother never admitted her sexuality to me.

And my father only did so late in his life.

It makes me wonder what else they kept from me and how their true selves might have impacted my upbringing.

It also makes me wonder if you know everything about your family. I don't mean secrets, but just basic stories that have been passed on through the generations. Often, children do not learn more about their families until they are older and begin to care about such a thing, but you died young, possibly before you could sit down with your father to listen to the tales.

You put much importance on education, stressing that your siblings remain focused on school and learning. That is a trait passed on to you.

In case you never heard this story, I will tell it to you now.

Your grandparents, Sheldrick and Nancy Burk, could read and write but never had the opportunity to receive a formal education because they were raised in the nation's pioneering years when families were more focused on obtaining land and establishing lives.

So, it was very important that their children attend school.

But there was one problem, a major one. There was not a school nearby. The closest was too far to travel during the cold winter months. So, your uncle James decided to start a school nearby for his nieces and nephews and another 20 or so children in the area. He opened it in a log courthouse in Wilkes County, Georgia and held classes there during the summer months.

Except, your grandfather died shortly after your uncle made that announcement, leaving your grandmother to raise a large family and run the farm on her own. It was a lot for her to handle on top of the grief of losing the love of her life.

Still, a few short months later, when the school opened, your grandmother sent the three oldest children, who she could have used at home. She refused to let heartache and a hard road get in the way of their education.

"Maybe they wouldn't be the smartest, best children in the school," your grandmother supposedly said, "but they are mine, and I know they'll do their best."

That started a tradition that you'll be proud to know lives on today: Education is stressed.

I did not receive a formal college education. It was by my choice. But I received an informal college level education at the dinner table.

Washington D.C. is not just capital of the United States. It is the political capital of the world, with diplomats and ambassadors and think tanks from around the globe descending upon it. Back then, I didn't understand why, nor did I question it, but those types of people often made appearances at my home for dinner. They discussed world affairs on an intellectual level, included me in the conversations and did not dumb it down one bit. By the time I was 10, I had a Ph.D. level understanding of world affairs, in my opinion at least.

One of the more frequent guests was a cousin's husband who was dean of students at George Washington University. I think he was the youngest ever appointed to that important position.

My mother's brother also dined with us regularly. He was an economics professor at George Washington University and was selected to represent our nation at an economic summit in Russia. Can you imagine that? I ate dinner with that guy.

Back to my parents and their secret, well, one of their secrets.

They divorced shortly after I graduated high school, and my father began spending more time in Maine.

Probably around 1993, I paid him a visit. I don't remember what we were discussing, but I guarantee his admission came out of the blue. He told me he was gay. Well, bisexual, actually, he said, since he'd obviously had relations with a woman.

It shocked me, yet it didn't. I somehow knew.

But I didn't press for more information or seek to continue that line of conversation. I was not comfortable at all talking about that with my father.

Probably a year or two later, during a visit with my mother, she confirmed that my father was being honest. I again don't recall what we were discussing, and it was again out of the blue, but she said, "Well, the problem with your father was he could never stay away from those men."

After my father died, my cousin, who was close with him, confirmed it yet again and told me how my father's sexuality impacted his life by costing him a government career.

As for my mother, it was her worst kept secret that she never told. Nearly everyone knew yet never spoke of it.

At one point she lived with a woman whom I was certain was her partner.

My mother had a heart attack in the 1990s. After visiting her hospital room, I recall leaving with a different cousin and asking if her "partner" had been to see her. My tone was clear that by "partner" I meant "romantic partner." My cousin said she was not sure but did not debate my accusation.

Then, in 2003, my mother had a stroke. I hired two live-in nurses to take care of her. They quit a few months later, only telling me that they refused to work for a lesbian on religious grounds.

I wonder why my father was comfortable sharing his secret, but my mother was not.

I wonder how many secrets my mother had.

Back to that stroke.

I don't know why I felt compelled to tell her.

Maybe I was worried she was going to die, and it was my last chance to do so.

Maybe I figured that since she was bedridden, she was a captive audience.

Regardless of the reason, I tried to tell her what happened to me as a kid.

I tried.

But all I was able to get out was, "Mom, when I was little, I was abused."

That was the end of it.

She covered her ears and began screaming, "No, no, no" on and on and on until I stopped trying to talk.

I had never seen her behave like that. I had never seen her so emotional.

It was bothersome, but I also didn't think too much of it at the time.

Years later, as I write this, I wonder … did she know? She seemed like she knew what I was going to say.

Your affectionate nephew,

Ben.

LETTER 17

Camp Sam Jones

Feb. 6ᵗʰ, 1862

Dear father,

As Mr. A.J. Chambless is going to start to Ga. this morning, I concluded to write you a few lines to let you know how I am getting along. I am in very good health at the present. However, it is not necessary for me to tell you any thing about the proceedings of the war; for he can tell you more about it then I can write.

A word to you Ma & sisters, E., M., and S., I would be very glad to have you send me a box of provision: such as sausage, potatoes, butter, lard, preserves, and cakes by Mr. Chambless that is, if you have not sent them already. I intended to have sent you 20 or 25 dollars by Mr. C., but have not drawn yet. We will draw in a short time, after which, I shall send you the above named amount. When we draw; we will draw $51 each of which, I can very easily send you $20 or $25.

Dear mother, I see no chance to get off home this winter, I therefore, shall make no effort.¹

Give my love to all the family.

Your affectionate son,
H. C. Kendrick.

P.S. you will please send me two packages of invelops, as it is a very difficult matter to get them here.
H.C.K.

---

1   Both the Confederate and Union armies provided furloughs. They could only be granted by company's commanding officer and were not granted to everyone who applied.

LETTER 17 REPLY

Dear H.C.,

I forgot to mention one of my father's favorite wartimes memories.

While in London, he stayed with the Clark family. They provided him with a bedroom in their house and all the comforts of home.

He only visited the base for his clerical work and meals.

The Clarks also fed him, but my dad said the Clark's had trouble finding certain foods as the nation recovered from the war. So, he preferred to eat at the mess hall rather than taking the Clarks' limited food.

Your last letter reminded me of his story.

My father loved to tell me about the time he was in the mess hall and spotted a basket of beautiful oranges with nary a brown spot. He grabbed one to go, put it in his pocket for later but forgot about it until he returned to the Clark's house.

When he pulled it from his pocket, my dad noticed Mrs. Clark eyeing the orange like it was a glass of water in the middle of the desert. So, he tossed her the fruit.

After catching it, he said she sniffed it like a rose and broke down crying.

Because of the war, she had not had an orange in years.

She called her husband into the kitchen, split the orange between them and then hugged my father.

I love that story.

I am happy that your family took such good care of you.

Your affectionate nephew,

Ben

LETTER 18

Dear father,

With the greatest interest, I take my seat to drop you a few lines; as I have a very pleasant time for it.

I have not received a letter from you in some considerable length of time. It is however, not necessary for me to mention any thing of that kind; for the transportation of letters, is so uncertain, that I have no idea that you get half of my letters.

Father, there is some news afloat; but I do not think it reliable, from the fact, that there are so many rumors passing at all times which prove false. It is reported here, that since old Gen. Beauregard left here, to go down in "Ky." that he had a contest with the yankees and give them scissors. We heard that he took 1,500 prisoners, the number killed was not given, and took an enormous number of horses and several other things which would be folly to mention. We do not believe it here.

We get newspapers every day or two here. In which, we find irreliable news, consequently, we believe nothing we hear until it is confirmed at least the 2^D time.

Father, we have been whiped several times since the winter commenced. I may be wrong; but I am inclined to think, that our great men have not discharged their duty in all senses of the demands that are made of them.

Here at Centerville, we are better fortified than we are at any other place in the Southern Confederacy, and there are more troops at this point than any other place in the South, and I think from the reason that I have just stated, there ought to be more at other points. The yankees would not have succeeded so well if we had not given them so much the advantage of us. They have been striking us on the weak points, by which means, they have whiped us.

It is reported here, that the yankees are advancing on us at this point, but it is not well founded; for it is impossible for them to come here yet, a while the roads are very bad. They are now covered with snow and sleet. It is sleeting now. It is also reported, that they [are] advancing on Winchester; and we have very few troops there. We did think here for a while, that we would have to go to that point; but I do not think we will have to go there for sometime if we have to go at all.[1]

Father, I want to make a request through you of brother Thomas, as it seems that I can't get a letter to him. It is this: If it will be agreeable with him, when his time is up which will be in a short time, I would like him after he shall have stayed at home 2 or 3 months, to come and take my place for a little while. That is, if it will not distract his arrangements. If he intends to join the army any how, I reckon he would as soon take my place as not. If he will do that, I think we will both be binefited; from the fact that it will be the only way by which, we can get a furlough to go home. We will reciprocate.

I do not know, that I have any thing more of interest to write. You must write to me as often as consistent to do so.

My health is very good.

Your son,

H. C. Kendrick

---

1   H.C. is reading the temperature of the war rather correctly, rumors are just that, rumors. There is much confusion on both Union and Confederate forces. Union-McClellan ignores the order issued from President Lincoln in January of 1862. Lincoln is forced to reorganize. Reassigns McClellan to Mount attack on Richmond, but this is not until March 1862. Confederacy – Davis is displeased with P.G.T. Beauregard and forces him to be transferred to Columbus, Kentucky in January 1862. He arrives by February 1862 to assist with the Kentucky Campaign.

LETTER 18 REPLY

Dear H.C.,

I haven't told you everything about my family.

I haven't told you why I really relate with your second mother.

I'm currently in a long-term relationship, but I have been previously married.

I was 22 and scraping by in the Arlington construction industry when we met in the mid-1970s. She was 10 years my elder and had six children from a previous marriage. I enjoyed her company but had no desire to marry her. I did not want an immediate family that included six children.

Then, in March 1980, she came to me with news. No, it was THE news. She was pregnant and, yes, the baby was mine. I had to do the right thing. I proposed, spent my life's savings on a small home and we married.

This is where things get weird.

The day after our nuptials, she told me she was taking a trip to her native country in South America to collect an inheritance from her father. It was welcome news, but also out of the blue. She had never mentioned this inheritance before. Not once.

Two of her children were adults and on their own, so I moved the other four into the new home and got us settled in, awaiting her return. A day became two. Two became a week. And then two.

Two weeks after she'd left, she called. She owed money in back taxes on the inheritance and could not leave or collect it until it was paid. So, I wired her the money.

Two months later, she called again, this time with news that our son had been born.

A month later, she finally returned with my son but without the inheritance. It was tied up in real estate, she told me. But that wasn't the biggest mystery on my mind. If my son was born in June, he would have been conceived in September. So, why did she wait until March to tell me and why didn't she look pregnant when she'd left for South America?

We later moved to Tampa, where I established myself as a contractor.

And, as my son grew older, I began to question if I was his biological father.

A barber noticed someone was dying my son's hair lighter when he was around 8. It was being lightened to better match my own.

I once confided in a friend that I wondered about the biological relationship. My friend and his wife agreed that I should.

My wife and I commenced a divorce in 2002. My son was a grown man by then, so I shared my doubts with him. He didn't get angry. He agreed I could be correct.

I traveled to South America for answers. There, I found the home where my wife stayed on the extended trip and where my son was born, according to his birth record. The homeowner told me that a baby had never been born there but did recall my wife telling them that she had given birth to a baby.

My ex-wife had told me her father was a police officer, I learned he worked in hospital and there was never an inheritance. Her father had died broke.

Back home, my son and I took a DNA test. It backed what we already suspected. We were not biologically related. My ex-wife refused to take a DNA test and she never has. I remain in the dark.

In this last letter you sent, you were questioning the validity of the truths you were told by the Confederacy.

You were wise to not believe everything you read when your eyes and ears told you otherwise.

There are always those who tell you what you need to hear to get you to do what they want. Lies could come from anywhere. From your government. From your military leaders. Even from family.

The Confederate media of course wanted you to believe that you were winning. Learning the truth might have caused the soldiers to stop fighting and dying for the cause.

You entered this war with your eyes wide shut.

By the time you sent this letter, they were beginning to open to the truth.

As for my son. Yes, he is MY son, just as your second mother saw you as HER son.

While we would both like to know the full truth, the truth we know did not impact our relationship. He is my son. I am his dad. And we love one another as though we are connected by blood and DNA, just as your second mother does you.

Your nephew,

Ben

LETTER 19

Orange Court House
April 8ᵗʰ, 1862

Dear parents & family,
I received your letters at the arrival of our recruits, and also, the boxes which were sent by them. You have no idea how well pleased I was with them. They suited me precisely. Notwithstanding, I get nothing of that kind here, unless it is sent from home, and although I am never so well pleased with them, and so much appreciate them, I would advise you not to send any more boxes or provisions of any kind.

My reasons for saying what I do, are these: The boxes cost more than they are worth, that is, by the time they get here, and after getting here, they do me but very little good. You very well know my disposition, that it is of such a nature, that I will give away every thing before one person should stand around me wanting what I have. Well, after having made a division of my little morceau,¹ that I got from home among 50 or 60 men, but a small portion remains for me.

I don't feel disposed for my parents and sisters to put themselves to so much trouble, and be at so much expense, and benefit me so little. Consequently, would advise you not to send any more. I feel however, that I must tender you my most earnest, serious, and unfeigned thanks for the kindness you have fairly shown to me since I have been out here. Well, I can, say this much: I will know when I get back, precisely how to appreciate good parents and love good sisters.

Col. E.R. Goulding is dead. Died very suddenly.² After his death, the regiment was marched up to Orange Court House to escort him to the cars. 3 men were sent to attend him home.

---

1   Morceau is defined as a short literary or musical composition. H.C., whom we can derive from the collection of letters is a learned young man; he refers to his packages from home as a small literary, or even to complement his family even more, a small musical composition.

2   Colonel Edwin Ross Goulding died of disease April 4, 1862, age 40. Prior to the war he was a Lumber businessman in Talbot County, Georgia.

The election for another Col. will be held tomorrow. I am in great hopes that Lieut. Col.[3] will be elected. He is a very clever man. In fact, he has been in command of the regiment all the time almost since we have been in the service.

As it does not become me to give you a full description of his death and his life since we have been out, I must forbear. I have reference to Col. Goulding.

Well, I reckon you would like to hear something about the proceedings of the war. I would like very much to give you a correct idea; but can't. They are absolutely in the dark. However, the report is now, that the enemy is approaching, but they will meet with great difficulty in their approach. And it has been said by the General, that we would have a contest with the enemy in a short time, but I think, that it will be at least a month before they can possibly get here. A full development of that fact has been made long since.

We are now about 70 miles from Centerville. We are in 1 1/2 miles of old President Maderson's[4] house, I saw his monument the other day, it is about 20 feet high.

Dr. Childs has been appointed our assistant surgeon. His office ranks with a captain's. I think he will do well for that business. As I have no more paper, I will have to close for this time, you will excuse me for not writing more.

Tell cousin Levisa Maddox[5] I have not received a letter from her yet. I have written twice, but will write again soon.

Give my love to all the family and friends, especially to her.

Your most affectionate son & brother,
H. C. Kendrick

---

3   The election of officers took place on April 15th. Lieutenant Colonel Richard Augustus Turnipseed was elected colonel. Resigned on July 26, 1862. After the war was a Lawyer, Farmer, Judge, and Georgia State Senator. Died in Fort Gaines, Georgia, November 21, 1900, age 70.

4   James Madison was the fourth president of the United States. His home was in Montpelier in Orange County, Virginia. It is still there as a memorial to the former president plus the more than 100 who were enslaved on the property.

5   Author's great-grandmother, Levicie Green Maddox, from Georgia. She was the fiancé to H.C.

LETTER 19 REPLY

Dear H.C.,

Are you aware of the difference between a hobo, a tramp, and a bum?

If not, I will now explain. Hobos travel and work, tramps travel and abstain from work, and bums do neither. There you have it.

So, when it comes to the homeless, the hobo is "King of the Road." When I was a child there was a popular singer, Roger Miller, who had a hit song of that title. A favorite of mine. Hobos don't beg or steal fulltime for a living. They work. Hobos, when I was a child at least, travelled the nation, either by hitching a ride on the train or putting their thumbs in the air and getting a car ride from a trusting stranger.

I told you earlier that a hobo jungle was near my house, in the woods along the train tracks. As you got closer, you could always smell what they called mulligan stew, which was comprised of whatever meat and vegetables various hobos could cobble together and toss in a community pot.

The Black hobos never made their way into my neighborhood. It was one thing to see a white hobo walking the street but, in those days, a Black hobo would have been instantly arrested, or worse if a racist resident saw him before law enforcement did.

One day, my friend's older brother heard which abandoned building nearby had become an evening home to a Black hobo. He gathered up a group of us and had us convinced we had to go down there to take care of that hobo just in case he decided to come into our neighborhood.

I was not racist. I neither hated nor feared Black people. But, for some reason, I agreed to tag along. Peer pressure is a thing.

We found the Black hobo sleeping in the building and pummeled him with rocks. I remember feeling bad as I tossed each rock but could not stop myself from throwing more. We stopped before any major damage was inflicted, but he was hurt, nonetheless. And, as we left, my friend's brother congratulated us on protecting the neighborhood.

Despite looking for work, white hobos were not above panhandling, and they did so as a unit. They would obtain chalk and draw a tiny line in the street in front of the residence if they knew a specific home was willing to provide food.

Well, we never gave out food, but someone must have erroneously put a line in front of our home one day.

I had to be about 4 years old. We were living in the basement of the multi-apartment home my parents owned, when the doorbell rang while we were eating dinner.

I ran to answer the door and found a hobo standing there, asking for some bread.

I took him by the hand and led him inside to the dinner table.

My parents did not want to squash my kindness, so prepared the man a plate before sending him on his way.

I am happy to read that things changed among your regiment. Earlier, you wrote that every man was for himself. Now, there seemed to be camaraderie and sharing, and it seemed that you were leading by example. Adversity challenges a soul and your perspectives have changed for the good, in less than 8 months.

It seems we have something in common H.C. I too prefer to give away everything before one person should stand around me wanting what I have.

I must be honest, though. A year or so after I was attacked, my attitude toward the hobos changed. When that home looked empty from that point on, I figured my attacker was a hobo who broke into the home to use it as a headquarters and then disappeared on the train, never to be seen in my neighborhood again.

I was wrong.

I later learned the identity of my attacker.

But I'm not ready to discuss that yet.

Your most affectionate nephew,

Ben

LETTER 20

Savana, Ga.[1]

August 8th, 1862

Dear father,

As I want to see brother R.S. & sister Nancy, I would like you [to] come down to see Thomas. He is too bad off to be left by him-self. I hate to leave him, but under the circumstances, I will have to do it. That is, if I get to see brother Robert.

He wants to see you very much indeed. He will not at all be willing for me to leave him unless you come. He is confined to his bed all the time; he can hardly sit up long enough to eat a little soup. I want you to come sure for Thomas will need some one when I leave him.

I have nothing of interest to write this morning.

Mr. Samiel Mills is here this morning, he expects to stay until Sunday. By that time, Thomas and Richard will be better, if the boys get better, I will come home with him. (Mr. Mills).

Pa., Thomas wants you to bring him some chickens to eat. There is a lady on the opposite side of the street that serve them up for him.

Be sure you come to see Thomas. Richard Mills is doing very well.

Your son,
H. C. Kendrick

---

1   Note the location. H.C. is home on a furlough. Between the time of H.C.'s last letter, about three months' time, 4 battles are fought – Siege of Yorktown, Battle of Williamsburg, Seven Days Battles, and Battle of Malvern Hill. Colonel Turnipseed resigns, July 26, 1862, following the last battle. Captain Benjamin Beck was elected colonel on August 1, 1862. H.C. and his Regiment took part in these battles.

LETTER 20 REPLY

Dear H.C.,

As strange as this might sound, there was something exhilarating about surviving that monster's basement. I wasn't aware of it then, but I was as I grew older. As a kid, I felt like I got away with something. I should have died. And that pushed me to the edge. For a while, I wasn't afraid of anything. I was not even afraid of dying. After all, I figured, I was living on borrowed time.

It must have been hard to watch your brother suffer.

He eventually did get better and returned to war.

He also survived the war. I am sure that you are aware of that. Then again, how would I know what the dead know and do not know? In case you do not know what happened to your brothers, let me fill you in.

As you know, despite pleading with your younger siblings to remain home, none listened. All five of your father's sons and two sons-in-law joined the Confederate Army.

John was never heard from again. To this day, we do not know his fate. Last reported John was living along the Red River working river boats when he joined up, according to a letter he sent back home.

Joe, your sister Sarah's husband, was the first to return, though family history says he was 'broken in health.'

Robert returned in June 1865 - haggard from having to walk all the way from Virginia, making him the second to return.

Cal, your sister Nancy's husband returned.

Then came Bennie, who informed the family that he'd heard Tommy was dead. A few days later a neighbor who served in the War confirmed his death. Bennie heard wrong. The family was still mourning when Tommy returned home, turning their sadness into the ultimate celebration. Tommy had been captured in North Carolina and sent to the Point Lookout prison camp in Maryland. After the surrender at Appomattox, Tommy was released and walked back to Talbot County, Georgia.

Bennie, my namesake, did not fare too well upon his return. After all, he enlisted around his 15th birthday, and returned home in 1865, as an 18-year-old war veteran.

He survived the war, but family history says he never was the same.

Great things were expected of him before he joined the Confederate effort. But he returned home with no career ambitions. He seemed to have no ambition at all, other than drinking and having a wild time.

Maybe that was a good thing. Maybe, after being on the verge of death for the duration of the war, he realized that life is short and to embrace every day as though it is the last.

But it was more likely what we now call Post Traumatic Stress Disorder, or PTSD. I believe they called it shellshock or neurasthenia in your day.

That brings me to Captain Goulding's death.

I think he might have been dealing with PTSD while still serving in the war. Goulding's life was defined by war.

Prior to the Civil War, Goulding fought in the Mexican-American War, a conflict often ignored in American history. The United States did not lose as many soldiers as they did in your war or either World War I or II, but over 15 percent of the soldiers died in the Mexican-American War, which is a higher percentage than either World War.

The Mexican-American War might also have been the United States' original sin, the first foreign war during which our soldiers committed atrocities on civilians – hanging them, raping them, burning their villages.

I cannot imagine what Goulding witnessed or was ordered to do.

He might have returned home, ready for a quiet life, hoping to put the nightmare behind him, only to be dragged into an even bloodier conflict a little more than a decade later.

I understand PTSD. I certainly had it. I was a bit of a menace due to my PTSD. No, I was a total menace. Two or three years after I was inside that monster's basement, I decided to run away.

At the time, I didn't know why I wanted to run away from home, but, looking back, I wanted to run away from that neighborhood. There were nights that I couldn't sleep, wondering if that monster was coming back for me. I'd been raped and he threatened to cut off my penis and kill my parents. I wanted to live in a place where I felt I was safe.

A friend said he'd run away with me, despite having no idea why I wanted to leave and himself having no reason to want to leave. We decided to spend our first night camping inside a sewage pipe at the local concrete plant. We collected bottles and, for fun, blasted them against a wall.

Our actions got the attention of the night watchman, who chased us from the premises but did not turn around once we were gone. He continued pursuit, pulled his pistol and screamed that he would shoot us if we did not stop.

He couldn't have caught us. We were halfway across a bridge and could have easily gotten away. But my friend froze at the mention of the gun, and stood there on the bridge, allowing himself to be caught. I could have kept running, but I didn't have the heart, so turned myself in too.

He brought us back to the plant and locked us in a bathroom and said he would have killed both of is if we were Black, but he used the racial slur instead. He then called our parents.

My friend was crying, partly from the fear that he was almost shot and partly because he knew he would be getting into trouble. He had every right to cry. Most boys of that age would have cried. But I didn't. Something was broken in me.

As the years went on, the PTSD benefited me.

Memories of the abuse faded. I recalled it happened, but the details were pushed into the recess of my mind. The anger was still there. The angst was still there. But the reason behind it was not as clear as when I was a child.

That's a good thing and a bad thing.

These letters are bringing those memories back.

That's also a good thing and a bad thing.

Your nephew,

Ben

LETTER 21

Winchester, Frederick Co. Va.

Sept 15th, 1862

Dear parents,

Over 12 months have elapsed since I sat in this old house to communicate to you my travels. Now I am in the same old place I wrote you the 2nd letter.[1] My heart was gladdened when I got in sight of this place. I was detained a good deal on my way to this place. I stopped one day in Linchburg, 2 days and nights in Richmond, but got along very well. When I got to Rapidan Station, I had to walk from there to Winchester, which is 75 miles.

You may know, I was tired when I got here. My feet were sore. When I was in Linchburg some body stold my shoes. I was bare footed for 2 days and nights. It was done on Saturday night, which left me to trot all day Sunday without any shoes. But on Monday evening I managed to obtain a good house to stay in, and on Tuesday I got me a pair of shoes. They were very good, better than the pair I left home with, but I was troubled a great deal in getting them.[2]

If I had nothing to do, but to speculate on shoes, I could make as much money as I would need all my life in 12 months. The common old negro shoes in Richmond, are worth from 6 to 10 dollars. I priced some there in the private stores in Richmond of the quality of them I brought from home, and it $15 cash. I told him (the owner), it was ridiculous to sell any thing at such exorbatant prices. He said he couldn't do better. But I went to the quarter master's office and purchased them from

---

1   The second letter was dated from Darkesville, which is around 17 miles from Winchester. Perhaps a letter is missing. Perhaps he wrote the letter from the home in Winchester but mailed it from Darkesville. Confederate soldiers were quartered in Winchester homes when the town was under their control.

2   This is H.C.'s third pair of shoes.

the government at 4 ½ dollars. So my feet are well prepared to take any of the hardships of a camp life.

I have walked 75 miles and will start to Frederick City in Meriland this evening about 50 miles from this place. My Regt. is there. It seems strange that I come around here but I couldn't do better as the yanks clash into Manassas occasionally and take our men. We have had a great many of our men taken there since we left there with our forces. They found out by some means, that we were going up there in small squads and would dash into the place and take these little squads of men. Having heard of this, at Culpepper Court House, I took Alexandria and Winchester Turnpike and came to this place.

Our forces, or at least Jackson's Division[3], came up to Harper's Ferry to catch some yanks that were there, I do not know whether he has succeeded in baging them or not. We hear canons there.

Company (E) 9th Regiment Georgia Volunteers,

Camp I don't know.
We are forming brigades to march to Harper's ferry, or to Martinsburg near the Potomac. We can't go in smaller crowds than 3 or 4,000 in safety. The yanks have gotten at last between Harper's Ferry and Frederick, to bush whacking our men. So, we have to go in large numbers to protect our-selves against the enemy. We expect to give them battle before we get to our several Regiments. And I don't care how soon.

We will give the best we have if it comes in the way. I think that is the only way we will settle this contest, is hard fighting. I think now is the time to do it. I for one, will follow them as long as I can walk. But I think our forces will fall back from Merriland[4] if she doesn't join us with a good force. That however I think she will do.

---

3   Led by Gen. Stonewall Jackson, one of the Confederate Army's most respected commanders and charged with defending western Virginia.
4   H.C. is spelling Maryland a couple of different was – Mariland, Merriland. As well as Lynchburg – Linchburg.y

My Regt. was in the fight on the plains of Manassas.[5] I don't know whether it is true or not, but I heard that old General Anderson[6] says "They will do to depend upon." He could hardly get them out of it when they got in to it. (the fight)

I have not learned how they suffered yet. But to a great degree I guess, Col. Beck[7] was severely wounded. Lieut. Col. Monger[8] was slightly [wounded] in the head, Major Jones[9] severely in the arm in the elbow. Old Lieut. Col. Monger is in command of the Regt. He went home shortly after the Richmond battle and just did get back in time to take a part in the battle. He is that old brave fellow.

As the privates are not notorious for rank, I have heard nothing of them.

I wish I had been there to share the boys' fate.

Tell miss Ann Bidel I left the things she sent by me to the boys in Richmond as I couldn't get them to them. I left all the things in Richmond.

My health is good.

Give my love to all the family.

Your loving Son
H. C. Kendrick.

---

5   Second Battle of Manassas (Bull Run), August 28 thru 30, 1862. Georgia 9th suffered 12 killed, 116 wounded. Total forces engaged-125,000. Total killed, wounded, or missing of Union -14,462. Total killed, wounded, or missing of Confederate – 7,387.

6   There were seven brigadier generals in the Confederacy Army about this time frame. There are three that could be whom H.C. is referring: George T. "Tige" Anderson, who served in the 11th Georgia Infantry. Brigadier General Robert Heron "Fighting Dick" Anderson. The third, Brigadier General Robert H. Anderson, who served in the 5th Georgia Cavalry.

7   Colonel Benjamin Beck survived. Returned home, and was later forced to resign due to disability in 1864.

8   Lieutenant Colonel Jacob C. L. Mounger. Killed at Gettysburg, Pa., July 2, 1863.

9   Major William Jones took up the command of the 9th Georgia Infantry after the death of Colonel Mounger, on July 2, 1863, until he was wounded and was succeeded by Captain George Hillyer. (1835-1927)

LETTER 21 REPLY

Dear H.C.,

Let me tell you the story of why I moved to Florida.

This story ends on my 23rd birthday but begins when I was 22.

During the summer of that year, I had a great job laying bricks. It was great because it paid $8 an hour. Everything else about that job was miserable.

I was one of 25 working on the crew. I'd estimate that 22 of those workers were Black with the remaining three being white. The other white brick layers were accepted and treated well because they'd been there for a while. But, because I was new and white, the Black workers did not want me there. It was a coveted job, especially for a Black man during those racist times. They didn't hate me for personal reasons. They simply hated me because they wanted another Black man to get my job. They figured, and rightfully so, that there were plenty of companies that would hire me at such pay whereas that construction company was one of the few that would do so for a Black man.

So, the Black workers banded together to get me fired and replaced with a Black man. They told the boss that it was either fire me or they would all quit.

That was not a hard decision for my boss to make. Of course, he would rather have replaced one employee than 22.

But he did not want to fire me. Doing so would mean he had to pay me unemployment. Instead, he decided to force me to quit by verbally abusing me. For days, he rode me pretty hard. I'd make a small mistake that was easily corrected but he'd snap and call me the dumbest guy he'd ever met, screaming it loud enough for everyone to hear.

None of that bothered me. I needed a job and that one paid well. Plus, the whole sticks and stones thing.

Finally, the owner of the company got involved. He was a big, fat, greasy man who could barely squeeze into the Cadillac he'd drive to the worksites each day. At the end of one workday, he pulled up next to me as I was walking to my car and squeezed from his seat to address me. Tomorrow, he told me, I was to report to a different worksite, one that was a good two-hour drive away. He thought the threat of that daily drive would be enough to force me to quit. I just nodded with a yes sir. That infuriated him. After hurling curse words at me for a good minute, he flatly said, "We don't want you here. Don't you get it boy?" He then reached into his pocket for a wad of cash that he gave to me in exchange for not filing for unemployment.

I had money but not enough to last long. I needed a job.

I quickly found one working for a home construction company, but it paid $2 less an hour. Still, it was a job, so I took it.

My boss was probably the best carpenter I've ever known, so it was a good job in that respect. I learned a lot from him.

He was also the hardest working man I'd ever met, and he expected all of his employees to follow his example. He expected everyone to come to work on time and work every second of the day. He was willing to overlook experience in favor of work ethic. But when someone asked for a raise, he typically had the same reply. He'd knock a nail into a board with two clean hits and say he'd pay 50 cents more an hour once the person asking for a raise could do that.

One story, which occurred before I was hired, alleged that one employee would not stop complaining about the pay and was spending the majority of the day bad mouthing my boss. So, my boss quelled that rebellion by calmly walking to his old pickup truck, retrieving his bow, and firing an arrow into the man's back in a place that would injure but not kill. That best sums up that boss. Incidentally the project was being built on Beauregard Street in Alexandria, Va., named in memory of your "*Old General Beauregard*".

It was on the Beauregard St. Project that I decided to move to Florida. It was December 3, 1976, maybe one of the coldest days of that year, which is easy to remember because it was my birthday.

It was cold. Iced-cold. The wind was whipping. The sun was hidden. And I was three stories up on a scaffold made of an old primitive board as I installed a cornice on one of the structures that had giant icicles hanging from it. My day started at 7 A.M. An hour later, I was so cold that I wanted to cry and then quit. Simply because my toes hurt bad.

Two hours later, my boss called us down from the scaffold for a short break standing around an oil drum that was turned into a fire-pit. He then gave us each a shot of whiskey for added warmth and sent us back to work.

When I got home that night, my hands were so numb from the cold that I couldn't have picked up a coin from the floor. Rather than a shower, I soaked in a hot bath for hours, refreshing the water whenever it began to cool from scolding hot to lukewarm.

It took months before I had a full feeling in my feet. My toenails turned black and fell off. I definitely had minor frostbite.

It was then that I decided to move to Florida. I did so a few years later.

I tell you this story because I had the option to move from the cold to a warmer climate.

I had the option to quit my job.

You never had that option in war.

Each hard day was followed by another.

Breaks were few and far between.

When you were not battling soldiers, you were shoeless battling the cold, still marching from place to place.

H.C., I do not support the Confederate cause.

But I am in awe of your strength.

Your nephew,

Ben

LETTER 22

Camp Hard Times[1]
Sept 21st 62

Dear father,
It may be, that you can't make out to read my letter, but I will
write any how.

The Regt. has been in 4 fights and has lost a good many
men in all the engagements. You may be assured, that our
Capt. displayed a great deal of coolness in all the different
fights. He is the only man in our company who has been with
the company all the time. He got 4 bullet holes shotten through
his coat.

All the boys showed a great deal of gallantry in the engagements. Cole Buchanan was killed - shotten all to pieces.
He was struck in the abdomen, one of his legs was thrown on
one side of a tree and killed there with his body on the other.
He knew not what struck him. Isham Waldrop was shotten almost in twain. They were the only ones killed in the company.
William Powell was badly wounded in the arm and leg. Samuel Fuller was wounded in the arm not so badly. James Arrington was badly wounded in side. John Morgan in the leg,
John Denson in thigh, I am in such a hurry I can't take time
to mention all and get my letter off today. Joseph Hough was
not hurt though he did his best in battle to killed all the yanks.
Old Joe did well in the fight. Whit Cureton was not hurt.

I did not get there in time to take a part in the fight. I wish
I had. Hurrah for our boys of this brigade. Old General An-
derson says he wants all the names that were in this last fight.
He says they killed as many men as there were in his brigade.
He says he wants to send every name to his county in eulogy
for him to his relatives.

---

1   Unknown location, but we can assume by reading Civil War History,
they are heading north. Battle of Sharpsburg (Antietam) was September 17, 1862.
Battle of Fredericksburg to commence on December 13, 1862.

We have but 12 men in the company now. They are all well at present. I was glad to see all the boys. They say they were greatly holpen up when I got here. We are expecting a big fight now. Or at least in a few days.

As soon as I got to the company, we were ordered to move, and marched almost all night. Lacking about 2 hours all of which was well employed in sleeping you may be sure. We got up by day, and moved until nearly noon, at which place we now are stoped.

I am well at this time. Joseph Hough is well. Whit Cureton is well, and in fine spirits. Old Col. Levi Smith[2] was killed on the battlefield. Little Jesse Pye is not killed yet. He is one of the greatest boys in the south. Jesse Bateman is well and with us. He acted bravely in battle. Harrison Barns, Calvin White, were taken prisoners. Bonnie was wounded in hand. Tell this to old Mrs. Mitchell.

I can't write longer. The mail is about to leave.

Give my love to all.

Your son

H. C. Kendrick

P.S. tell A.D. Chambless that his case is all right with the Capt. Though his Certifficate has not been received. I told the Capt. He was not playing off.

---

2   Levi B. Smith was commissioned captain of Company K, 27th Georgia Infantry and was elected its first colonel in September 1861. A lawyer from Talbotton, Georgia. Killed in action during Battle of Sharpsburg, September 17, 1862.

LETTER 22 REPLY

Dear H.C.,

Carpentry can be a dangerous job. Do it long enough, and you'll likely lose at least a finger. All it takes is one slip up while operating a table saw and you'll live the rest of your days with nine digits instead of 10. Even the most experienced of carpenters have lost concentration and had such an accident. One lapse, even for a second, is all it takes.

In reading your letters, I find myself trying to put myself in your shoes or, at times, lack thereof. I am trying to find moments in my life that compare to yours, so that I can understand what you were going through.

But truth be told, nothing I experienced measured up to that damn brutal war you had to fight. Today, historians refer to the battle you reference in your last letter as either the Battle of Antietam or the Battle of Sharpsburg. Regardless of the name, the battle is considered a turning point in the war. It marked the Confederacy's first attempt to invade the north by moving into Maryland, but they were repelled by the Union. That gave President Abraham Lincoln the confidence to issue the preliminary Emancipation Proclamation warning the Southern states that he intended to free the enslaved. It remains the bloodiest day in U.S. history with 22,727 dead, wounded or missing in the fields, woods and roads of Sharpsburg, Maryland.

Some might say my childhood tragedy is equal to a bloody battle, but I don't believe so. Maybe it would be for some. I do not want to diminish what other such victims have endured. But, for me personally, it does not equate to fighting for survival 24/7 and watching friend after friend die or suffer a life altering war wound. Heck, after a lifetime of construction, I still have 10 fingers and no terrible scars, but perhaps that has more to do with luck.

Sometime in the 1980s, I worked in the Tampa shipyards owned by the Steinbrenners, a family perhaps best known today for owning the New York Yankees, a baseball team for whom you would likely not root.

I was hired as a carpenter for the ship building company, making $10.85 an hour, a wage that was hardly worth the risk. Four men died on the job during my short time there, a little more than a year.

I didn't see, but recalled the details of two of those deaths.

The yard had four drydocks and in between was a landing area to where equipment and supplies were delivered via an in-yard rail crane system. A crane would load whatever was needed from the landing area onto a ship being constructed. Those cranes could lift quite a bit of weight, but they also had limits. The crane could carry less when the boom was fully extended than when it was only partially. The crane was imbalanced if the weight limit was breached when the boom was fully extended.

On one day, the crane operator began arguing that they were asking him to lift too much. He'd have to extend the boom to its absolute apex for that particular job. The boss didn't want to hear it. Lift the damn weight, he said, or hit the road. Fine, the crane operator said, but you stand next to me on the running board, and the boss did. Well, the crane operator did as he was told. The crane did as he predicted. It toppled over. The driver and the boss died.

On another occasion, a ship's chain anchor was being lifted onto the dock. But the chain was piled poorly. Those chains are as heavy as they look. All it took was one link to be improperly piled on the dock. It slipped from the side and into the channel, it took the entire chain with it like a ripcord. A worker standing nearby got dragged down with it and died.

The final straw for me was when I was lit on fire.

I don't remember what I was installing, but it was in the engine room. During construction, that was one of the most hectic places to be. Workers were everywhere, crisscrossing and getting into one another's way as each sought to perform their particular job without enough care for what the others were doing. One of my coworkers joked saying, "We're like worms in the apple!"

In the room, a big diesel engine was located at the bottom of a 30-foot-deep pit with guardrails at the top to make it difficult for anyone to fall in. Well, as I mentioned earlier, it takes just one lapse in judgement. Two of us had a lapse that almost took my life. I lapsed when I decided to lean on the rail and look down at the engine for an extended period of time and did not pay attention to my surroundings. And a welder lapsed by wildly Air Carbon Arc Gouging a heavy piece of steel as he hung a few feet above my head with his helper nearby, ostensibly as a fire watch, and said nothing of the work above my head.

An orange ball of melted molten steel broke from whatever the welder was working on. It was small, but white hot. It dropped right on my hard hat, onto my neck and rolled under my shirt and stopped on my belt. Dancing around I ripped off my shirt just as it started to flame and melt, and shook off the piece of hot steel. (*I no longer wear synthetic clothing*) The scar it left on my back is minor, but still there.

I quit a few days later.

It takes a little bit of luck to retire as a carpenter without a major injury. It also takes the ability to walk away. I had money saved, so could afford to quit, and remain jobless for a few weeks. Others do not have that luxury.

You never had that luxury. Neither did William Powell, James Arrington, old Col. Levie Smith, or the others.

Your nephew,

Ben

LETTER 23

Dear father and family,
With cheerfulness, and gladness of heart this beautiful Saturday morning, my mind is directed to my good old home, and more especially to those by whose care it is kept.

Father, I can inform you of the fact this morning that I have at length obtained a position, which, to the point at which you have often wanted me to arrive, has a striking relation.

Now the question arises within you what that can be. It is one of not great importance, though, by it, I am relieved from a great deal of duty. not in my sphere, but in respect to the duties of those who only occupy the attention of a private's position. It is the position of 2nd Sergeant. My wages are 17 dollars a month. It is a better position than I had before I went home. The wages are better than before.

I am Sergt. of the guard today; but have stolen this opportunity to write you.

The Capt.[1] came to me the other morning, and told me he was going to get an instrument of writing from the Col. of the Regt.[2], which would, as well as bind me to my duties, give some showing for my position, so that if the Capt. should get killed or die, I cannot be thrown out of office by him. Who might take his. (the capt.'s place).

Father, I am doing as well as any soldier can do. I have been favored beyond a doubt. There have been no favors shown to a man in this war of my position, but that have been shown to me. Father; you and ma. need not suffer any uneasiness about me; for you may be assured, that if there are

---

1   By October of 1862 the 9th Georgia Infantry, serving under D. R. Jones' Division, was broken up and assigned to George T. Anderson's Brigade, Hood's Division, Longstreet's Command. Not sure who may be H.C.'s Captain?

2   Unsure whom this rank is, again due to the turnover and loss of higher rank officers.

any favors to be shown by the Capt. toward his men, I will be shown my portion.

Capt. R.P. Welborn[3] seems to think more of me, than any of his men. So be easy about me.

Pa, I think a great deal of Capt. Welborn.

Military duty hurries me.

Give my love to all the family.

Your loving son

H. C. Kendrick

P.S. Mr. Harvey is going to start back to GA. in a few days, and I will send this letter by him. I would send you the money I promised you, but we have not drawn yet.

Our camp is pleasant. The days are cool and pleasant, the nights are not too cool for us.

I can't tell anything about the movements of the military.

As I promised to give you some idea of the health of the valley boys, I will do so. Joe Hough, and Whit Cureton, Sam Harrison, Henry Peed, James Drue, are well and look well.

Good by for this time.

H.C.K.

Bill Powell is dead. John Denson too.

---

3   Robert P. Welborn was elected captain January 1, 1862. Killed in battle at Knoxville, Tennessee, November 19, 1863, age 23.

LETTER 23 REPLY

Dear H.C.,

Among the secrets I learned about my mother through her records after she died was that she almost married another man. He worked at Dave Taylor Model Basin with her. She broke up with him in 1952 and married my father just months later.

You were proud of your promotion, as well you should have been. You likely earned the higher rank and the respect of your captain. You deserved all the accolades.

I must wonder if my parents' marriage was about love or promotions.

As I mentioned in a previous letter, they were both gay.

My father lost his job during what was known today as the "Lavender Scare."

To explain the Lavender Scare, I should first back up and explain the "Red Scare."

The Red Scare was the fear that Russian communism would infiltrate every facet of our government and society in order to undermine our nation from within. That scare peaked in the early 1950s when Senator Joseph McCarthy began investigating anyone accused of being communist. Some accusations were true. Most were false, based on hearsay, rumors, and lies.

Hearings were held. The accused had their names dragged through the mud. Many lost their careers and good names even though they were absolutely innocent.

The Lavender Scare was an offshoot of that movement.

Washington D.C. and Arlington had a population explosion after World War II with many returning soldiers, like my father, moving there in search of federal jobs. And, some, like my father, were gay. Thus, a gay community began to flourish there.

This frightened the powers that be. They were concerned that a homosexual would be too easy to blackmail. They foresaw communists threatening to expose gay government employees unless they turned on their country.

When faced with that fear, the government could have advocated for gay rights and told the masses that being homosexual is absolutely normal. That would have solved the Lavender Scare. No one could have been blackmailed if homosexuality was accepted. But, instead, the government doubled down and declared homosexuality to be a mental disease that had to be purged.

Just like they did to accused communists, the government investigated anyone rumored to be gay and fired them for the slightest reason.

Other times, they'd stake out gay bars in search of government employees.

It was a horrific and sad time in American history.

My father was among those purged.

Anyway, back to my mother and back to those boxes of records she left behind.

There were probably 30 or 40 boxes, and, in retrospect, those were part of my inheritance. She never spoke much about her past, but those boxes told me quite a bit about it after she died. I wonder if that was purposeful. I like to think it was.

Still, I initially looked at those boxes as garbage and a nuisance and actually threw some out before, for whatever reason, I became riddled with guilt and decided to look through them.

That's when I found an old newsletter from her days at David Taylor Model Basin. Each newsletter provided the normal workplace updates you can expect but also profiled employees and included personal announcements. One such announcement mentioned that my mother and a fellow employee had become engaged. I was blown away by that revelation. My mother had never mentioned any of that to me. Then again, I rationalized, she never told me anything about herself.

I kept digging through the boxes for more and discovered letters and a diary entry that told me more. Apparently, her first fiancé changed after the engagement. He became possessive and wanted her to quit the workforce to stay at home full-time.

So, my mother left him.

Not long after, she and my father ran off to California to wed. That's all I know about their romance. I don't know how they met or why they married.

It makes me wonder, did my father believe a marriage would convince the government that he was not gay and that he would get a second chance? Did my mother marry my father because it was more convenient than marrying a heterosexual? Did she marry only to pretend she was heterosexual? Was there any true love between them? I wonder, did the government believe my mother or did they choose to pretend along with her?

I wish I knew.

Your loving nephew,

Ben

LETTER 24

Oct 8*th*, 1862
[Near Winchester Va]

Dear brother,

As I am idle this morning, I will write you. Don't think that I never make any effort to effect an opportunity of writing you because I say I am idle, and for that reason, I will write you; For every time my duty will allow of my absence, I will and have been writing to you or someone else of the family ever since I have been here.

Communication is almost entirely cut off; but thank the one to whom thanks are due, there is a mail occasionally yet. I expect Bennie, you think I have slighted you since I have been out here. I will say, that when a letter is sent by me to any one of the family, it may, and I hope will be considered as including the whole of the family. You may be assured, that my intentions are good if they are not carried into effect.

We have moved a mile nearer Winchester than we were three days ago for the purpose of joining General J.B. Hood's[1] division to which we are now attached. General D.R. Jones[2] is gone home on a 50-day furlough. I don't like General Hood as well as I like'd Jones. He has already issued some [very, very] ridged orders. which are not at all agreeable with my notions under the circumstances. They are these: We are not allowed to leave the limits of the brigade which of course would not be at all hard if we could get enough to eat, but we don't get enough to eat by nearly half. We get five biscuits for 2 days all of which can be eaten in one day by a hearty man. If we could peruse the country, we could get a good deal to eat from the citizens.

---

1   Despite rapid promotions, John B. Hood was also known for high losses among his men.

2   General David Rumph Jones. Promoted to Major General after the Battle of Antietam. May have never returned from his furlough, died January 19, 1863, suffered from a lingering illness.

Now you may think that I am discouraged, because I write thus; but not so, for I am as cheerful as you are knowing this to be the fate of warfare. It is not because we have not gotten the provision in the confederacy; But it can't be brought to us.

We are in five miles of Winchester. We are still without tents, and I don't expect to have any more shortly if. ever. I have had the best health since I have been out the last time, that I ever had in my life. I am almost afraid that I am going to be sick, my health is so good. I haven't felt at pain since I have been in Virginia the last time.

I must close for the present.

My love to all.

Your brother
H. C. Kendrick.

Write to me Bennie.

P.S. Now, I have just returned off a long general review. It is almost night, and I will be compelled to go to bed to night without anything to eat. You will probably have something good to eat, but your brother will not have anything at all. We will draw something tomorrow morning, but it will be nothing but five biscuits and 1/3 lb. of beef for 2 days.

This isn't the first time we have done without dinner, supper, or breakfast. It is some suffering to be hungry, but not so much as to cause death. I have always thought, that if I could live, I would not make any fuss. I am glad I am yet [alive][3].

Good by brother,

Yours,
H.C.K.

---

3   Author has made an assumption here, word appears in crease of letter and difficult to read.

LETTER 24 REPLY

Dear H.C.,

In the mid-1980s, I applied for a construction job with Pacific Architects & Engineers, which was similar, yet dissimilar, to the one on Ascension Island. I believe the job paid around $70,000, which is a ton of money at the moment that I write this letter, and, even more back then. What's more, it was a tax-free paycheck if you were out of the United States for an extended period.

The job was at the American Embassy in Russia. It was the height of the Cold War and our government suspected that our embassy was full of hidden listening devices placed there by Russia in hopes of acquiring secrets for the Russian government.

Information is power.

To better understand, perhaps I first need to explain that this job was likely overseen by the CIA for the State Department.

The CIA – the Central Intelligence Agency – is our nation's foreign intelligence service. Or, to put it more bluntly, our international spies.

The CIA formed after World War II as part of our nation's strategy to remain a superpower. They are a standing army that is also invisible, formed to ostensibly protect democracy.

Their network extends beyond the government agency. They also work with what are referred to as department of defense contractors, which are companies they sometimes may hire to secretly do their dirty work. In this way, the CIA can ensure that a covert job is done but can claim ignorance if the plan is blown up. For instance, they might work with a publishing company that primarily works with literature related to foreign militaries. This allows certain employees to use that as cover to get on to foreign bases and gather information for the CIA. Or they might work with a foreign hotel management company that allows the CIA to bug certain rooms where certain people are staying.

The job for which I was interviewed was to rebuild whatever was destroyed in the search for the listening devices. I'd be working for a construction company hired by our government and, in my opinion, that company was likely connected to the CIA. So, who knows how much of the job description was true? Maybe once I arrived in Russia, they'd have me doing something else, like build things to cover listening devices our country installed so as to record conversations between our ambassadors and those visiting them. Maybe my job was to do exactly for what the job description called, while fellow employees carried out more covert missions. Maybe there was nothing clandestine going on. Who knows? But the experience drove home the CIA's greatest weapon – information.

As part of my interview process, I had to meet with a government official at his Tampa, Florida hotel room. He called me at home at around 7 P.M. on a Thursday night, and with no wiggle room, asked me to be at his room within the hour.

He answered the door moments after I knocked, and I almost fell backwards when I saw his face. He looked almost exactly like Clarence Odbody, the angel in the beloved Christmas movie "It's a Wonderful Life." I wonder if you know about that movie, if spirits follow such things. If not, you will have to trust me; that it is a wonderful story and a classic that most Americans know and love.

Anyway, he invited me in, had me sit on the couch and began asking me a series of odd questions. He didn't want to know about my work experience or anything like that. He instead asked if I ever did drugs, about my sexual preferences, criminal past, things like that.

As I answered each question – I tried drugs when I was a teenager but nothing further, heterosexual, and no major arrests – he looked inside a notebook, possibly because he already had the answers. I think he was just checking my honesty.

He then got a little too personal and, in my opinion, crass. I won't repeat exactly what he asked. I will only say that he inquired about specific sexual acts and used language not for church.

I finally snapped and asked, "Why the hell he needed to know about this kind of crap?"

"Blackmail", he said. He needed to be certain that I didn't have skeletons in my closet that the Russians could use to blackmail me into supporting their side.

Blackmail? But all I was supposedly doing was building things. What secrets could I have learned that I could have shared? What information could I have collected for the Russians even if I was blackmailed?

But I was not hired, so I never learned the truth.

Information is power.

During your war, food was power.

You were hungry for a reason.

The Union Army cut off the supply routes to prevent food from getting to the Confederates and destroyed food producing plantations. The Union also imposed blockades on Southern maritime ports. The Confederate government asked for cotton plantations to grow more food, but too many young men were off to war to work the farms or oversee those they enslaved. Some enslaved worked less or not at all. Others fled to the Union. This was a concerted effort by the Union to starve the South into submission.

In your time, food was power.

But, in my lifetime, information is power.

Your nephew,

Ben

P.S. *"I have always thought, that if I could live, I would not make any fuss. I am glad I am yet alive."* Amen to that uncle.

LETTER 25

Dear parents,

Captain R.P. Welborn is going to start home tomorrow, and I expect he will come to your house before he returns, if not, you will get intelligence where to send my clothing to for him to bring to me. If Capt Welborn comes to your house, I want you to remember, he is one of my best friends, and I want you to treat him as such. I have no better friend in the world, save you my dear parents, than Capt Welborn. He has proven it since I have been with him in the service, and you may be well assured, he will do to depend upon for an officer in battle.

Mother, you know what to send me. You need not send me any thing but winter clothes, a coat, pair of pants, socks however, I don't know, that you need put your-self to any trouble to send socks. You can judge for me better than I can for my-self.

I am doing well as can be expected of a soldier. We get nearly enough to eat now. I buy some flour and meat to help me in rations. The health of the company is good, that is those who are here. Robert Lumkin's health is not good at all. But with that exception it is good.

Capt Welborn will notify Mr Chambless to find out the families who wish to send clothes by Capt W. You will please tell old Wm. Brooks to assist in going round to find the families, to inform them of his coming. So that, they can prepare to send the clothes to the boys.

Tell Miss Ann Bidel that Capt W. will bring the boys their clothes I brought to Richmond, to the company. He will be furnished transportation for them. I must close.

Give my love to the family.

Don't forget to receive Capt W. with all the cordiality of your son's best friend.

Your loving son,

H. C. Kendrick.

LETTER 25 REPLY

Dear H.C.

Company E, 9th Regiment, Georgia Volunteer Infantry also known as The Talbot Guards was one of 10 companies that comprised the regiment. Company E seemed to be exclusively formed of men from Talbot County. It also elected many of its officers. I imagine you knew many of the men and their families. With that said, there must have been much pressure on you to do your best as to not let anyone down back home. The network of families back home reciprocated and showed their gratitude by supporting the troops.

Washington D.C. metro area where I was raised, which is what I refer to as: The Capital of the World (by default). Is a transient city. I was not transient. I met many people who were transient, only there for a certain term. There are some families who have been there for generations. But I was not one of them either, because my parents moved there, to make a career. As a result of moving around the city I developed friendships with people from the various branches of service, elected officials, businesses that work for the government, people representing foreign entities, and then the local government and business.

Many of my friends' fathers were high-ranking officers, and many were war heroes from World War II. Other friends' parents were congressmen. As a child and even as a young adult I never realized how unique it is to be raised in that type of environment. I actually believed when I was young that the whole country was like D.C. One thing we did not have, and that was a cradle-to+grave cohesive community as you did.. In a way I envy your Talbot County because of that.

Chris, perhaps only a few miles from where you were stationed in Northern Virginia near where your regiment fought, there is a road called the Beltway it is about 60 miles long with maybe 10 lanes for traffic, it circles the city like a belt. Today there is a derogatory term for the people who live within its boundaries "Beltway Insiders" or worse "Beltway Bandits". I was not one of them even though I did live inside the Beltway.

The term was coined to describe the powerful forces in Washington that many Americans do not have faith in and believe are double-dealing away the collective assets of our country. Politically speaking things have not changed much since your day. Cohesion is powerful and even more so when *"liberty and justice for all,"* is the *rule* of law.

By the way, one of my childhood friends went on to become lieutenant General in the army. I had forgotten about him and saw it in the news. Your letters seem to be rattling a lot of my memories loose.

Your loving nephew,

Ben

LETTER 26

Dear father and family,
After a long delay, I have at length taken my pen in hand to write you. I have not been careless with regard to writing to you. You may think, I have grown obstinate and indifferent about my relatives at home; but not so, for you know, if you will take the second thought of my character, that my happiness consists greatly in writing to, and receiving letters from my friends at home.

Father, my reasons for not writing sooner, are good I think.

In the 1ST place, I have had no chance within the last 3 weeks to write,

2^D, I have not had any paper on which to write,

3^D , I haven't had anything to write with,

these are the several reasons why I haven't written, all of which are correct. You, I know, will be satisfied about it when you consider the circumstances under which I am placed.

Five days ago, I was 125 miles from this place. We were ordered to move to this place last Wednesday, on which day, we started for this place. We had a very hard march of it indeed.

The first day, we marched 23 miles during which day we waded the Shenandoah River. The weather was very cold, the river about 2 ½ feet deep, the number of rocks incalculable and very sharp. We prepared to cross, then pitched into it heartily. It seemed that the water would cut our legs off. I never had water hurt me as badly in my life as that did. I pulled my shoes off my feet and took it bare footed. My feet hurt me so badly I came very nearly crying. I reckon you think me somewhat childish, but it is the fact, if my feet had hurt me any worse, I should have cried sure. This was the 1st day.

On Thursday morning early we started on our way to this place. Soon in the morning, we had to cross the same river again. Where it was about 300 yds. wide and 2 ½ feet deep. You may know, from my experience I did not draw my shoes off. I didn't suffer as much the 2D time as I did the 1st. This ends the river sensation.

We proceeded onward all the day until 4 o,clock when we stoped to camp. So we continued on until my feet got so sore, I could scarcely walk but I kept up as I always do under any, and all circumstances. I can walk as far as any one in the service of the confederate army.

I don't know where we will go, but I am inclined to think, we will go to Culpepper Court House. It is very uncertain about where we will go to from here. It is, and has been the talk, that we would go to Richmond; but circumstances go to show, that we will go to Culpepper.

You know father, the ways of war are wavering. We are all in high spirits. I think some of the boys believe, we are going to Ga., which is very prompting to them to be in high spirits. I would be glad that we could winter in Ga. close to home.

My health is good, and the health of the company is good. Joe Hough's health is good as usual.

Give my love to old Billie Brooks. Tell him I will attend to that business for him as soon as it will be available.

Write soon

Your loving son,
H. C. Kendrick.

LETTER 26 REPLY

Dear H.C.,

I've canoed the Shenandoah River before.

It was the early 1970s when I was in my early 20s and I was with a friend who was even crazier than I was.

We shared a two-man aluminum canoe. It was not the strongest vessel. The river was way too high that day. It was right after a rainstorm, so had to be nearly 13 feet higher than average, and we planned on paddling one of the more notorious sections of the body of water, an area known as the staircase because the rocks are in a staircase formation. In short, we should not have attempted to conquer it that day. But we tried.

Because the water was high, it was also fast. We dropped our canoe in, paddled a short distance, and then got caught up in the current. Our canoe shot down the river like a bullet. We were so out of control that we both later admitted we considered jumping but realized that would be even more dangerous.

And then – BOOM!

We hit a rock, but we didn't bounce off it and keep going. Instead, the canoe was partially stuck on it. We couldn't move as the fast-moving water funneled inside the canoe while our paddles floated to the shore. We stupidly swam for the paddles, nearly drowning in the process, and then sought to return to the canoe. I'm not sure what we thought we could do with the canoe. Were we going to bail the water from the canoe as it kept flowing in? Somehow lift the heavy canoe from the water? We had no plan. It didn't matter.

The canoe was against the rock like a kindling stick over the knee prior to breaking. We struggled against odds but managed to free the canoe, after which we resumed our adventure and headed into the confluence of the Shenandoah and Potomac Rivers. We were unaware of the turbulence that lay ahead, created by heavy rain, the first wave of water hit our bent canoe and filled it in seconds. Exhausted, wet, and moving at a good rate of speed, we paddled towards the south shore and reached land in about a half mile. There we met some friends who helped us drag the bent canoe up to the road and back to safety.

We did all of this without life vests or helmets.

We easily could have died.

You wondered if you sounded childish in reliving your ordeal on the Shenandoah River.

There is nothing childish about that river.

I learned the hard way and it was summer.

Your loving nephew,

Ben

LETTER 27

Camp near Orange C.H. Va.
November 15th, 1862

Dear father,

I have not heard from home since I left. The mail however, is so uncertain, that I would not pretend to say you have not written. I haven't a doubt, that you have written though, I haven't received it.

I have written several letters since I have been here. I am getting exceedingly anxious to hear from home. Since I wrote you last, we have moved toward Culpeper C.H. about 16 miles. We are now within 6 miles of Orange Court House. I see no evidence of leaving here now. We will probably be here for some time yet.

I heard Gen. Anderson say the other day, that there was a very good prospect of going to Ga. in a short time. I am very anxious to go there, though I don't know that we would be binefitted a great deal by it, for I am of the opinion, that if we go to Ga., we will have a great deal of hard duty to do. There is, of course, some object of importance [!] In view if we are sent. We don't get a great deal of good news here. We are excluded from the privilege of getting any newspapers at all, therefore, we are unable to get any news of much importance. We learned the other day, however, that Gen. Jackson whipped the enemy from the Shenandoah river.[1]

We also heard that Gen. Stewart[2] had been fighting 4 or 5 day with them on the lines, but that is of but very little value.

---

1 The Shenandoah Valley Campaign took place in the Summer of 1862, the Maryland Campaign, Antietam and South Mountain Battle took place in September of 1862. Is H.C. receiving news of these campaigns?

2 James Ewell Brown Stuart, "J.E.B." , or "Jeb", was a Confederate Cavalry Officer. Considered one of General Robert E. Lee's most trusted men, calling

The cavelry fighting is of but little avail. About all the good they do, is watching on the lines for the purpose of giving intelligence to them who do the fighting, they are principly the infantry.

We have heard, that the enemy is advancing on Petersburg, and that 20,000 had landed at city point below Richmond, but I don't think it is true. Still, it may be so. I don't think we will go to Ga., though, it may be so.

We haven't any tents yet, neither do I think we will get any at all. We all enjoy good health. We get enough to eat to make out on. I can't say we get enough to satisfy our appetites, but we can live. I reckon it is the best for us, not to get enough to eat for I believe we are fatter than usual.

We don't draw any soap now at all, but the way I get my clothes washed, I carry them to some lady in the country and have them washed. I find it to be a difficult matter to keep hands clean without soap. I am very well fixed in the way of clothing. I drew a pair of new shoes the other day.

Father, I will send you some money as soon as I can send it by hand. It is too precious to risk by letter.

Father, as I consider it due to him, I will send you the obituary of W.B. Powell. If you find any place in it where you can better it will please do so.

I must close. Give my love to the family.

Your son.

H. C. Kendrick

You will please have this obituary published in some newspaper. I have writen it for the binefit of his parents.

Obituary of W.B. Powell.

On or about the 29th of August 1862 W.B. Powell, one of my military comrads in the company I belong to, while in the full discharge of his military duties on the battlefield of Manassas,

---

him the "eyes of the army." Mortally wounded at Yellow Tavern, near Richmond, Va., May 12, 1864, aged 31.

was shotten through the arm and, while endeavoring to get to the rear another bullet struck him in the leg which at once disabled him.

He was picked up immediately and carried where he could obtain medical aid. When he got to the Dr., all the medical aid thought necessary for his case, was administered. He was then sent to the Hospital at Warrenton where he though well attended to, died.

Departed this life _____ ³of Sept 1862, W.B. Powell, son of Thomas Powell of Talbot Co. Georgia, after having received a severe wound in the battle of Manassas.

I having been at home at the time he was shotten, did not see him, but am well assured that he was in high spirits, and in the earnest and vigorous prosecution of his duties as a soldier. But alas, alas, how soon was the news changed!

That terrific agent took hold of him which so often bids defiance to all human sagacity and the best medical skill – which rejects every bribe which fair promises can offer, and heeds not the entreaties, or claims of doing right, or protecting house, home and sustaining all that is noble, right, and just, blasted every fond earthly hope. This should be the chief concern of all who engage in battle, that is, to be prepared for such a struggle.

He was preeminently an honest man, modest and as retiring as could well be of a man of his age. He was but little known beyond the circles of his business relations, and that of his immediate friends; but there he was known, respected and beloved to a degree that seldom falls to the lot of any young man. In paying a tribute of respect to any one who has gone to number among the dead, it is due to him as a faithful soldier, to record his virtues.

There is in the life of an independent and honest man something so worthy of imitation; something that so commends itself to the approbation of others, that his name should not be left in oblivion.

---

3   H.C. left a blank here in the letter, for he did not know the exact day.

Mr P. had not professed religion; but always had a high respect for it; especially as it was so greatly exemplified in his good mother and kind sisters. I have often heard him speak of so well loving his kind sisters, and good mother because of their religious punctuality. As a young man of business, he was punctual, just and honorable – as a son reverential and obedient – as a brother, kind and confiding. Honor and prudence marked his life. On first entering the service of the Confederate States, he resolved to resist all imprudence. From the time he entered the war, until he died, he sustained this resolve.

We hope all the young men in the war observe this rule, and be as punctual to their dutys [duties][4] as Mr. W. P. was before he died. Let our soldiers have their minds placed upon heavenly things; that when their lot shall be to die. Whether by the deadly stroke of the bullet or from the effects of a worn out body, be prepared to rise above terrestrial pleasures, and be ready to enter the celestial joys of heaven.

H.C.K.

---

4   H.C. corrects himself here and transposes over the top of his error, such the scholar.

LETTER 27 REPLY

Dear H.C.
Due to your words, you can be assured your friend's name is not left in oblivion.

Ben

LETTER 28

Camp near Fredericksburg Va
November 26th, 1862

Dear father,
With cheerfulness of heart this morning I take this opportunity of writing you.

I guess you wish to [know where] I am, 4 miles from Fredericksburg. We are stationed here for the purpose of taking charge of a battery.[1]

The enemy threatened to bombard the city some 2 or 3 days ago but have not made the attempt, yet our cars were fired upon the other day.[2] The enemy knocked a box off the back with a cannon ball, not doing much damage, however. Old General Burnside[3] of the Federal fleet ordered the citizens, that is the women and children, to leave the city, which they did with haste.

We had a very hard march before getting here. A march of 61 miles, which we accomplished in 3 days. It was raining a good deal of the time. I got thoroughly wet to the skin, which rendered me very unpleasant indeed.

Our pickets are within 200 yards of the enemy's pickets. There is but very little firing on the picket line. I am not disposed to think there will be any fighting done at this point. I think the Yanks entered to have us raise our forces up here

---

1   This becomes known as the Battle of Fredericksburg, fought December 11 through 15, 1862. A Union defeat. Total forces engaged: 201,000 Confederate 78,000 killed, wounded, missing- 6000 Union 123,000 killed, wounded, missing 12,500 (Battlefields.org)

2   Sounds as if he has been aboard a train.

3   Major General Ambrose Everett Burnside, Union. Known for many battle losses, as well as casualties, he was reassigned. On April 15, 1865, he resigned. After the war held directorships for several railroads, and later became a three-one-year-term-time governor of Rhode Island. (Battlefields.org) (Wikipedia)

while they will be getting off somewhere else in order, to strike in a weak place. I reckon they will hardly do it without our knowledge. I hardly think, we will have to fight up here this season. I am willing to do it if it will do any good, for I am anxious for this very wearisome war[4]

---

4   The remainder of the letter is missing.

LETTER 28 REPLY

Dear H.C.,

In downtown Tampa, Florida in 1911, the city erected a statue honoring the Confederate cause.

Or, at least, that is what they said was the statue's mission.

The statue depicted two Confederate soldiers – one heading toward battle to the North and the other walking home to the South.

Such statues were erected throughout the South during that era in U.S. history, but half the country believes the monuments had a nefarious meaning. During this time, Black men, women, and children were beginning to establish their own communities. They owned property. They were accumulating wealth. Some believe white Southerners grew jealous, so erected Confederate statues to remind the Black residents to remain in line or face consequences.

To accentuate that point, Tampa historians long pointed out that, at the statue's dedication, a keynote speaker said that Blacks were an "ignorant and inferior race."[1]

It all came to a head in 2017 when Tampa area residents demanded that the statue be removed from its home outside the county courthouse.[2] It became a hotbed issue. Men and women on both sides of the debate spoke up at public meetings for weeks.

Those in favor of keeping the statue continued to say it honored those who fought for the Confederacy and, regardless of your opinion on the war, it was part of our nation's history and should not be erased.

Those in favor of removing the statue continued to point out its racist roots, reminding the public that it was erected to intim-

---

1   Contorno, S. (2017, June 17). For Tampa's Confederate Monument Racist History Clouds Claims of Heritage, *Tampa Bay Times*.
2   Contorno, S. (2018, March 21). Confederate Monument Has Quiet Start at New Brandon Home, *Tampa Bay Times*.

idate and was also a symbol of a hateful America that once embraced slavery.

The statue was ultimately moved to a less populated area outside of Tampa.

Meanwhile, such debates were going on throughout the country. Some Confederate statues were destroyed or removed. Others stayed put. Sometimes, the debates grew violent.[3]

But it became more than an issue debated in localities throughout the nation. It became a national issue with national leaders taking sides, loudly advocating for their point of view, and demonizing those who disagreed. Their rhetoric turned what could have been a civil debate on the legacy of those statues into a debate fueled by bile and hatred for the other side.

And then, those same leaders used that issue as an election platform and to fundraise.

Do you see what was happening? Did you watch this from your vantage point?

They did not care about the actual issue.

They only saw it as a tool to divide our nation and to keep themselves in power.

"Elect me," they screamed, "or the enemy will come for you!"

The best way for demagogues to remain in power is by dividing the populace and demonizing those who do not agree with them.

It's true now. It was true during the Civil War.

The remainder of your letter is missing, but I will guess that the next words you wrote were "to end."

I wonder how you feel knowing that the war has never really ended. It just transitioned from the battlefield to city halls and state capitols. It still resides in the hearts and minds of the many generations that followed. Resolution of a conflict is challenging especially when there is a lack of will.

Would you be proud that the South has never really fully conceded?

Or would you wish that the wearisome war would just end and for our nation to finally come together.

I personally wish this very wearisome war to end.

3   Cox, K. (2021, April 12). Black Protesters Have been Rallying Against Confederate Statues For Generations, *Smithsonian Magazine.*

Your nephew,

Ben

P.S. Chris, I attended two different high schools, one named for the Union Navy Admiral David Farragut (now closed), and the other for Confederate General J.E.B. Stuart (school name has now been changed).

LETTER 29

Camp near Fredericksburg Va
Dec. 6th, 1862

Dear father,

I received your letter which was sent my Capt. Welborn yesterday. Capt. W. has returned the same day.

Tell Ma., I got my clothes she sent by him. Tell her, they suit me exactly. She could not have pleased me better if I had been there. They came on the right time to facilitate me for duty. I must acknowledge my gratitude to her for them. Ma, you shall be compensated for it if it is in my power to do so. You must receive my thanks, you, and sister E. for your kindness to me. I don't know what I should have done if it had not been for the clothes you sent me. Ma, and sister, you will please accept my small compensation.

I was glad to hear of brother R.S. I wish it may be that he may not be exchanged, because he is so much needed at home.

We have just come off picket guard. We had a bad time, but not so hard as the Regt. which is on picket at the present. It snowed all night last night, which renders the weather unpleasant today. There is no probability of leaving here shortly though, the place at which we have to stand picket, is very disagreeable. It is in 30 feet of the water of the river, which makes the place much colder than it would otherwise be.

Pa, I want you to tell Sam Fuller to write to me. Tell him that I miss him more than any body in the company. I want to learn how he is getting along. I think I can imagine about how he feels when he goes to bed at night and gets up in the morn. He feels as it were, like a partridge out of cage.

I don't think there will be any more military operations of noterity up here this winter. The weather is getting so inclement, that prudence would not suggest a forward movement of either party. Artillery can't be used to any advantage at all, upon which, the yanks principally depend.

The health of the company, is good at present. We have 62 men on camps out of which, 45 are for duty, 4 on extra duty, the rest complaining a little.

Joe Hough is well. Tell Mrs. Hough, I did not bring his clothes she sent by me to him. I did not think it would be prudent and safe to do so. I will try to get W. Powell's cloths to Benjamin P as soon as I can.

I will send $15,00 cts to Ma, sis E. and sister Sarah to Ma, for sending my cloths.

To sis E. the same for assistance, sis S. for that she loaned to me before I left home.

My health is good. My love to all.

Your son

I will send you some in my next letter. This is enough for one letter.

H. C. Kendrick.

LETTER 29 REPLY

Dear H.C.,

I'd like to tell you one other story about Ascension Island, this time about its inhabitants.

We called them "The Saints" because they were originally from Saint Helena.[1]

They were the most unusual and beautiful people I have ever seen. Rumor has it they are a mix of those who had visited Saint Helena over generations – Chinese, Indian, African, and European. Some had mesmerizing, gorgeous brown skin, blondish brown hair, and striking blue eyes. The contrast was crazy.

The Saints were pretty much sequestered on Saint Helena, bound to the island. It was difficult for them to leave the island, yet they didn't have much of a future on the island, at least by American standards. They weren't going to Harvard or Yale or Oxford or Cambridge or somewhere like that. Still, I stress "by American standards." Many were happy on their tiny island and their simple, relaxing, and paradisaic lives. For those who were not content, it was a dream to get work on Ascension Island more than 700 miles away.

Today, I hear there are hundreds of Saints on the island. But back when I was there, I recall 50 or 60. Back then, they earned $2 an hour doing the same work that paid me $13 an hour. But that $2 was a fortune to them. And seeing anywhere but Saint Helena seemed like an adventure to them.

They were happy. Ascension Island was their land of opportunity.

They loved the American culture.

They had this tiny radio that they used to blare country music as they worked. Boy did they love American country music.

1   Saint Helena is an island in the South Atlantic Ocean, a Territory of retain. Napolean Bonaparte was exiled there in 1815, after the Battle of Waterloo.

But they loved Ron Jon Surf Shop more.

Ron Jon Surf Shop is a chain of tourist shops that sell surfboards and surfer clothing and beach souvenirs. Government workers would often visit the island wearing a Ron Jon hat and shirt. To The Saints, Ron Jon represented American culture and they wanted to represent it.

It's due to The Saints that I understand how exciting it must have been for you to receive those packages from home.

I planned a long flight to Cocoa Beach, Florida, a one week break from work.

Cocoa Beach had a Ron Jon Surf Shop. When The Saints learned of my destination, a few wanted me to bring them back a Ron Jon shirt.

A handful of them each gave me $20, a quarter of their weekly pay. I felt so guilty and wanted to talk them out of it, but they were grown men.

I went to Cocoa Beach, and as promised, came back with a box full of shirts. Well, they were lined up waiting for their shirts before I stepped off that plane. You should have seen their excitement as I opened the box and tossed them each a shirt.

I've never seen anyone more appreciative for anything in my life.

I guess life is all about perspective.

Then again, your family knows all about that.

I love your family's origin story.

Your grandparents, Sheldrick Kendrick and Nancy Burks, were awarded more than 200 acres of land after the removal of the Cherokee and Muskogee indigenous peoples in Baldwin County, Georgia via the 1805 land lottery. When your grandparents arrived at their homestead, all that the county had at that time was dirt trails that had been cleared through the thick foliage. They ultimately constructed themselves a family compound that could comfortably fit their six children and anyone who needed a place to stay for an extended period of time when passing through. But, early on, all your grandparents had was a lean-to next to the covered wagon that took them the 77 miles there from their previous home in Wilkes County, Georgia. But rather than complain about what little they had, your grandparents would marvel at the weather they enjoyed and the stars they gazed upon each night.

Their children, including your father, also later made do with what little they had. Your father's favorite childhood possession was supposedly a slate with a pencil attached that he enjoyed hiding like treasure in a hole in a base of a tree that he and his sister covered with a board.

And then there was a time your family was struck with tragedy. After your grandfather suddenly died and your grandmother had to raise six children on her own, as the story goes, she looked over her sleeping children one night and thought to herself, "Yes, I still have something for which to be thankful."

I love that story.

Perspective is important.

Ben

LETTER 30

Dear father,

My opinion given in my last has proven erroneous.

Last Thursday the 11th of this month, we were aroused by the awakening noise of canon 1 ½ hours before day. We were ordered to get ready to move by the dawn of day. At which time, we were formed in line to march. We marched out into an old field and halted - stayed there about 1 hour - drew 60 rounds of cartridges and moved up the river 3/4 of a mile in the direction of the canon, which as we moved on, became more furious. We when we got within 1 mile of the Yanks, halted, formed a line of battle behind an old fence now. We stayed there until night.

When we, that is our regt., was ordered to go on picket guard down on the river's side. We went to the river, each company of the regt. to its post. About 10 o'clock in the night, one of General Anderson's staff, came to us and told us to move from there, to leave 10 men and 3 noncommissioned officers and a commissioned officer to hold the place if it could be done easily if not, to get away if they could.

About ½ an hour after we had left, 4 or 5 men (I.E., yanks) came down the river in a little flat to find out as we suppose, our position. The 10 men of ours who were left there to hold the place, fired on them very rapidly so much so, they were compelled to seek a landing place on the other side of the river. At the time of the fire, we were lying in a little pine thicket ½ mile distant from it.

We were then ordered to form a line of battle at the same point we had been lying during the day. We lay there all night without any fire. I did not get cold however. At the dawn of day, we moved up the river ¾ of mile at which place we formed another line of battle in a little piece of woods. Stayed there about 1 hour, and then we moved out and went up the river ¾ of a mile however, A. P. Hill's[1] division took the place of ours immediately after we left. And stayed there until we could form a line. We stayed at this point one night.

At the dawn of the 13th day, we were ordered to move farther in front of our line at that time. We went down across a vast plain until we got within 600 yds. of the enemy when we halted behind a little ridge about like a dry ditch, and formed another line opposite A. P. Hill's division on our right. Here was a nice point with us as we all believed the yanks were advancing with apparently a great deal of determination, but when they got within 400 yds. of our skirmishers they halted, the same as to say we had better hold on a while and find out more about the rebels' position. Thus we remained until 11 o'clock in the day, when all at once the yanks advanced on A.P. Hill's division with tremendous fury and determination.

Now the ball opened on our right with great fury. We lay perfectly still. Our attention occasionally drawn off by the singing of a minie ball shotten by the yanks at our skirmishers passing immediately over our heads. Not hurting any of us however. The battle raged with the greatest fury I ever saw in my life. Our division was not in it at all but the left of the fight was not 300 yds. from us. It lasted about 2 hours. The [yat][2] yanks broke our lines and their skirmishers got to our depot on the rail road, but were soon repulsed with great slaughter. We had the decided advantage of them. That is the reason so few of our men whiped so many of them.

---

1 Ambrose Powell Hill Jr., a Confederate Lieutenant general. Following Stonewall Jackson's death he commanded the Third Corps of General Lee's Army of Northern Virginia in the Gettysburg Campaign. Killed in action during The Third Battle of Petersburg, April 2, 1865, age 39.

2 Yat – H.C. seems to be using this word as slang and/or derogatory. Meanings found means female, nothing or nothing less. So maybe referring to the yanks as weak or nothing. (urbandictionary.com)

General Thom Cobb's brigade[3] drove back 3 or 4 brigs. of theirs. Thom Cobb was killed whose death is much lamented in his brigade. He was up on our left. The fight up there was more hotly contested than the one on our right. I must confess, that the yanks made the attack at the place to whip us if they had had the right kind of men and the blessings of God upon their side, but as that was not the case, we whiped them the worst kind.

General Lee[4] said he was highly pleased with the result of the day's work. We lost some 2500 men killed and wounded, the yat yanks 3 times as many. I am confident that the yanks were the worst beaten they ever have been yet. They came against us with at least 5 times as many as our own force. I never saw men in as high spirits as ours are at this time.

The yanks are supposed to be moving down the river. If it had not been for the river, we would have driven them back to an unanticipated point by them.

I am anxious for the war to close. I never felt more like fighting in my life than that day. I will be glad to see the time when this war of much suffering will close. Not only glad to see it close, but am willing to help close it.

The weather now is cold and disagreeable. The health of the company is good at present.

Tell Mrs. Hough Joe is well.

I forgot to tell you of the accidents of our brigade. The 8th Ga. 3 killed and several wounded. Ours, 2 or 3 wounded the 7th 2 or 3 killed.[5]

---

3   Thomas Reade Rootes Cobb, a Confederate Brigadier General, lawyer, author, politician, and ardent secessionist. One of the founders to The University of Georgia School of Law. Killed in action, December 13, 1862, during the Battle of Fredericksburg, age 39.

4   Robert E. Lee, commander of the Confederate States Army, taking full command on February 6, 1865. Surrendering at the Appomattox Court House on April 9, 1865, resulting in the end of the American Civil War. After the war he was appointed president of Washington College (Washington and Lee University) in Lexington, Virginia, from October 1865 – October 1870, age 63. (Wikipedia)

5   Battle of Fredericksburg Report of Casualties – Total Confederate Troops - 72,000; killed, wounded, missing - 5,309. Total Union Troops-114,000;

My love to all the family.

I have no more paper at the present, I am very cold. I must close. Write soon.

Your most affectionate son,
H. C. Kendrick.

I have no idea we will stay here long. My love to aunt S Trussell. I will write again soon.

killed, wounded, missing – 12, 653. (Wikipedia)

LETTER 30 REPLY

Dear H.C.,

Spurned by the government, my father had to find other ways to help my mother support the family.

One of his earliest jobs that I recall was working for the local donut shop called Donut Dinette. The job came with an old panel truck with a large donut painted on either side. I thought it was the coolest thing in the world and loved cruising through town with him, nodding to my friends with a boastful, "Yeah, my father works in a donut shop."

I am as astounded by the details in your letters to your father as I am about the ordeals you faced time and again. I wonder if you provided such details because it was therapeutic or because that was your relationship with your father – you told and shared all. And, if it was the latter, is it reciprocal?

My father, despite keeping his sexuality from me until I was an adult, was pretty much an open book with me. Likely, because we spent so much time together when he was working.

Pretty much all his jobs seemed cool to me.

At some point, he was also a host at the Water Gate Inn, a famous restaurant that served Pennsylvania Dutch food. All the local movers and shakers dined there, and my handsome and outgoing father was the perfect person to greet each at the door and show them to their seat. When I watched him work there, he seemed like a movie star.

After that, he owned his own restaurant, the Columbia Road Inn. I loved to sit on a counter stool and spin until I grew dizzy and ill. I also loved to guzzle creamers, again until I grew ill.

Later, he drove a cab. Then worked at a picture framing store that he eventually purchased when the owner retired. It also sold art supplies and brushes. Business there typically picked up after an election when new officials moved to D.C. Jackie Kennedy was among his customers, as was Lincoln Rockwell, founder of the American Nazi Party. Talk about a contrast.

What's odd is that it never struck me as odd that I knew so much about my father's careers, yet next to nothing at all about my mother's. I knew she worked for government contracted agencies and was good at math. That's all.

It turns out, the secrecy was likely by design.

Let me tell you a quick story about a hotel with which you might be familiar – the Greenbriar Hotel, established in 1778 in the state we now know as West Virginia. It's been known as "America's Resort," especially so during your time when five sitting presidents stayed there before you left for war.

During World War II, the hotel was used as a hospital for the soldiers. Then, after the war, the government secretly built a bunker under the hotel. Perhaps employing a thousand workers, all sworn to secrecy. That bunker was meant to house the U.S. Congress during a nuclear attack.

To care for the bunker in secret, the government had a shell company called Forsythe Associates that claimed that it maintained the hotel's televisions located in each room. That deception enabled government employees to walk the grounds without anyone wondering why. The secret was maintained until the *Washington Post* discovered and wrote about it in the 1990s.[1]

That story harkens back to my letter detailing the CIA's shell companies and explains why my mother was so secretive.

Forsythe was considered a Department of Defense contractor company.

Some of those perform such work openly. For instance, Boeing is publicly known for providing Air Force One to the president.

But others are contracted secretly, and their work is considered classified.

---

1   "The Ultimate Congressional Hideaway", Ted Gup, reporter, Washington Post, May 31, 1992.

And others are contracted openly, perform some work that is unclassified and other work that is classified.

Curtis Wright Aircraft Corp and David Taylor Model Basin both had public contracts with the government when my mother worked at each. But David Taylor Model Basin might have performed classified work too. I am not sure about Curtis Wright Aircraft Corp.

My mother had left David Taylor Model Basin before I was born.

While I grew up, all she ever said was that she worked as a computer programmer for companies that did work for our government. She never shared more.

Now I wonder, was that because her work was classified? If so, why?

But I am getting ahead of myself.

I'll explain more at another time.

My love to all,

Ben

LETTER 31

Dear parents,

Not having heard from you since my last letter, I have concluded, that you perhaps did not get it. I would not, however, hesitate to answer your letter twice - even if it were received. I would not be so ungrateful, as to stand upon writing twice to you, while I get one letter from you. It is with a degree of pleasure not often experienced by an ordinary mind that I write, from the fact, that while in these distant climes of destitution and disappointment, I am well satisfied, that my welfare is duly taken into consideration and that my eternal interest is not forgotten.

Before I further proceed, I am notified, that we will have a battalion drill in a few moments so I will stop until that is over.

I have returned from a most desparate drill ground. The nature of the field in which we drilled, is about like that old Lloyd field of yours.

Now, I proceed to give you a short sketch of my military life within the last 2 weeks.

On the 26th of Dec. we moved camp about 1 mile to get wood to burn. The proceedings of the military operations for the last 10 days, have not been very active, in fact, they have been more inactive than usual. Our pickets and the enemy's have been holding communication with each other until recently when they received orders from General R.E. Lee, for no communicating to be held between them. There are on both sides, some who are of no more firmness, than to give to each other intelligence of the most valuable importance.

We have the mildest weather for the time of the year I ever saw. This day however, is not so fair as they have heretofore been.

I am inclined to think, the enemy will not endeavor to affect a crossing of the river at this point again – as they made such a complete failure in the first effort. I don't know, that there will be any more maneuvering of importance done by either party this season. It is true, we have as good weather for military operations as we will probably ever have, but the certain expectation of the coming of inclement weather, prompts them to withhold a while. The enemy is doubtless discouraged at the present; from having been so much disturbed in their war department, and so sadly disappointed – in their certain anticipations of success.

My very kind parents will please excuse me for being short and uninteresting. I am not in the proper mood for writing a long letter today.

Give my very kind respects to brother R.S. Tell him, I will write to him shortly.

My love to all the family. Write to me soon.

I am your loving son,

H. C. Kendrick.

N.B. tell Ma., sister Sarah, and sister E., that I, in my letter writen on, or about the 6th of Dec., sent them 5 dollars each, and would like to hear from them concerning it.

H.C.K.

LETTER 31 REPLY

Dear H.C.,

In the mid-1990s I started a side company focused on importing construction wares from Latin America – certain types of wood for walls, certain ceiling, and floor tiles, stuff like that. It's work that, on occasion, sent me overseas to make new lines of distribution and finalize deals.

One such trip sent me to Central America.

An employee of mine for that business was from Central America, arriving in the United States as an illegal, who was brought here via a smuggler. When he heard I was visiting his homeland, he suggested I reach out to his friend for free room and board. The man had a nice house, I was told, and was always willing to accommodate friends and friends of friends.

So, I reached out and the friend invited me to stay with him. It was set.

Before driving to his home, I took my business meetings. And, during each meeting, when I mentioned where and with whom I was staying, I was met with blank stares, shaking heads and warnings.

That man may be a drug dealer, I was told, a leader of a cartel that imports massive quantities of drugs to the United States, through my home city of Tampa. With puzzled faces, I was told tacitly told to avoid him.

They had no reason to lie to me, but I had to be sure. So, I drove to the house. It was a mansion, a castle, with a thick and tall gate for security. It did not feel right. It confirmed to me the rumors were true, so I kept on driving, straight to a hotel. When I returned to Tampa and my employee asked about my stay, I made up some lie for why I never went.

> Our pickets and the enemies have been holding commu-
> nication with each other until recently when they received
> orders from General R.E. Lee, for no communicating to be
> held between them. There are on both sides, some who are
> of no more firmness, than to give to each other intelligence
> of the most valuable importance.

You never know who you can trust. That was true back then and
is just as true now.

Not long after I returned home, I attended a community meeting
in my neighborhood. Crime was growing out of control and drugs
were to blame. A police officer was there to listen to our concerns
and express what he and the department could do in conjunction
with our efforts.

When the meeting was over, I approached one officer and informed him of my trip to Central America and the intel I'd learned. I
gave him the cartel leader's name and asked if he knew of the man.
That cop's face changed, and he took a step back. "Those people are
bigger than us." he told me, tacitly suggesting I drop it. He gave me
the impression that he was scared.

I considered going to the feds myself, but then realized that they
would not care.

Back then, the United States was embroiled in what we called
The War on Drugs. It was a federal response to end the nation's drug
epidemic that was destroying our cities.

But they always seemed to go about it all wrong. They waged
war on and arrested the drug users and low-level drug dealers. Those
men and women then served long prison sentences. For many, their
only crime was addiction. And those selling drugs were doing so
for pennies on the dollar and were so far down the chain that they
were unknowingly supporting rich and violent cartel leaders in other
countries. Meanwhile, those cartel leaders and their top men and
women in the United States remained free and unbothered by law
enforcement.

There was good reason for this. Some of those cartel leaders
were working with the CIA. Their deal went like this: The CIA
looked the other way as the drugs were being smuggled into our
nation. In exchange, the cartels had to do battle with government of-

ficials in their nation that our government was against. Our nation's leaders were willing to poison a countless number of Americans and incarcerate others as a political weapon.

Our government had such deals with cartels and many reports have been made supporting those facts by media journalists for years.

Your Nephew,

Ben.

P.S. Chris, Danny Casalaro and Gary Webb were journalists who were investigating and reporting allegations of governmental involvement with organized crime. Both died by suicide, but rumors persist contrary to official reports. May these brave men rest in peace.

LETTER 32

Dear parents,

For the first, in the year of 63, I have made an effort to write you. I think, from this time hence I will, indeavor to write you once a week at least. The new year has broken upon us regardless of the circumstances under which we are placed, or the condition of our persons. I have it plainly demonstrated to me, that time, in making its rounds, has no reference to the preparation which man may have made to meet the coming incidents.

I thank God, however, that the year of 63, has found us in the best of health, and in the finest of spirits. I think every moment only brings peace and prosperity that much nearer to our beloved Southern Confederacy. I haven't a doubt, but that we (the people of the South), are destined to freedom, as the Christian is to inherit eternal bliss in a future State. It may, however, cost the lives of many good, gallant, and noble men, but the harder the trial, the sweeter the liberty.

God grant, that we may show that obedience and resignation to his will, which characterizes a high regard for, and a pure humility before God.

We have a dispatch here this morning, stating that general Bragg[1] has fallen back from Murfreesboro.[2] It seems, that he falls back every time he has a fight, which only serves to encourage the yanks and prolongs this disastrous war.

The yanks are fortifying at this place, but I think it all in vain. They will never be able to whip us from this point.

---

1   Braxton Bragg, commander of the Confederate Army of Mississippi, which later became the Army of Tennessee. Bragg was known to be the worst general and most unpopular of the Civil War. After the war was employed by various municipalities as an engineer of various public works. Died in 1876, age 59.
2   Battle of Murfreesboro, Tennessee began December 31, 1862, through January 2, 1863. Became know as one of the more intense engagements of the American Civil War.

Though, they may cause us to fall back by flanking us. Everything seems to be quiet on the picket line.

I will send you 10 dollars in this letter as I have not the chance to send it by hand. It seems that I will not have the opportunity to send you money by any than by letter. You will receive it.

Pa. my health is good the health of the company generally, is good. Joe Hough is well. Whit Cureton.

I will send you 10 dollars every month this year, if my health is good. Write soon. I haven't heard from you in some time. For my sake write to me.

Your very loving son,

H. C. Kendrick

LETTER 32 REPLY

Dear H.C.,

I actually have some military experience. I stress "some" but maybe even "some" is an overstatement.

One day in the summer of 1968, I came home from gallivanting around the neighborhood to find my suitcases packed. My father had news. I was being sent to military school in Tom's River, New Jersey a few hours north of our home, and we were leaving in the morning.

He didn't explain anything on that long quiet drive to Admiral Farragut Academy. He didn't have to. I was 14 at the time and still at my height of acting up and getting into trouble. My parents didn't know how to handle me or how to talk to me. And I didn't want to talk to my parents. I knew why I was so angry, but I also was too scared to tell them why. In the back of my mind I was still worried that monster from around the corner would kill them.

My father checked me in, gave me a sort-of hug and said his goodbyes, leaving me alone in a strange place.

I only stayed there for a year and really don't have any stories of interest to tell. I learned to march and stuff like that. That's about it. And the entire time, I wondered if my parents loved me. I felt alone and was depressed. Like you, I would wonder when they would write or call. They would, but not as often as I would have liked. For my sake, like you, I needed to hear and read their words.

Upon returning home, my parents enrolled me in a new school, where something strange happened. Somehow, by my junior year, I had nearly enough credits to graduate. All these years later, I am unclear why exactly, but I think it had something to do with taking accelerated classes at the academy and my parents pushing me for years to take extra classes at the local school that could be used toward my high school degree.

The school faculty didn't want to graduate me that young and toss me out into the real world, so they enrolled me in their Industrial Cooperative Program, otherwise known as ICT.

That program worked like this: I took two classes in the morning and then spent the rest of my day working a job that taught me a skill. I got a job and the school facilitated everything else. By entering this program, I could remain in high school until the end of my senior year. It was a way to slow down my graduation.

I found a job in the kitchen of a 300-bed hospital whose kitchen was run by the Marriott Corporation. I worked on a dish assembly line, scraping and scrubbing, and washing, and drying and so on.

It was a good enough job. But, a few weeks later, the kitchen manager, an Armed Forces veteran, complimented my work ethic and offered me a promotion. He was going to make me a cook.

His announcement was not welcomed by cheers. I thought he was picking on me. "Cook? That's a woman's job," I said. But he countered that I would be working with the chef and him, in fact, he said all the best chefs in the world are men. More importantly – I'd get a raise.

Sign me up!

The head cook was a big Black man from North Carolina. He had to be 10 years older than me, and he started working with Marriott through the ICT also. He later became one of the Marriott's first Black hotel managers, running one in Atlanta. Imagine that?

When I arrived on my first day, he stuck out his hand, as we shook he said "Nice to meet you." with sincerity. Because of his sterling social skills he was a pleasure to work with. I started with breakfast on a Saturday morning. I was cooking 60 scrambled eggs at a time on a giant grill for the patients, visitors, doctors, and nurses. From there, I learned how to make lunches and dinners for masses of people too. It was a great experience. I met quite a few girls working there. I was also introduced to drugs for the first time, just marijuana, nothing major, but didn't care for it one bit.

I stuck with the job for the school year and through the summer.

Then, during my senior year, with only one class left to take to graduate, my English teacher had another idea for me. She wasn't going to pass me, no matter what. I had a passing grade, she told me, but she didn't like my attitude and didn't trust that my transcripts were accurate. She didn't think there was any way that someone like me was as smart as my transcripts claimed. I tried to argue, but she didn't want to hear it. I was not going to receive a diploma from that school. PERIOD.

So, I stopped arguing and just walked out and went home.

I don't know what was wrong with that lady.

Maybe she wanted me to stand up to her.

Maybe she wanted me to prove that I wanted a diploma and demand that she pass me.

Maybe she just hated me.

Maybe she was miserable and sought company.

I never returned to school again.

I did manage to get my diploma.

Two or three years later, while visiting my father after his divorce from my mother, he handed it to me.

He never forgot what the school did to me. So, he secretly and forcefully lobbied for them to make it right. They finally gave in and graduated me, even though I was not one class short.

I guess that's how my dad showed love – through actions rather than words or hugs.

Looking back, I appreciate it.

Your very loving nephew,

Ben

LETTER 33

Dear parents:

Thinking, this letter would be productive of an answer, I assume the privilege of writing you a fifth time before having gotten one from you. You have certainly written to me since Capt. R. P. Welborn got back to Va., but I haven't received a letter from you since that time. If you haven't written to me, you will confer a great favor upon me by writing.

I received a letter from brother Thomas 5 days ago, which gave intelligence of the arrival of his regiment in Wilmington N. C. His letter stated, that he and brother Joseph were well. He says, he has just begun service.

There has been some talk of our regiments moving to that point, but I have no confidence in the report, that is, so far as this regiment is concerned. I have no idea but that some troops will be sent from this place to N.C., but as I have very dear relatives there, I flatter my-self with no such good luck.

On the morning of the 21st, we were awakened by the sound of their canons, which was supposed to be signal for some important move, and a prelude to a hasty march. Soon after the signal was given, orders came to us to be ready to move in a moment's warning. We fixed up our blankets, - got ready to move, and defied the yanks to approach.

While we were thus ready, confidence characterized every Southern countenance. The actions of our men indicated a willingness to meet the foe though the weather was cold and disagreeable. The following day told to us, the indisposition on the part of the yanks to cross the river. So it turned out to be not any thing of importance. This, however, serves only to make us more vigilant, and prompt to our post as soldiers.

There is nothing of value going on at present. I will not dare say, there will not be some important move shortly. My mental abilities are not capable of penetrating the dark cloud which intervenes between me, and the maneuvers of the military. I have, however, a right to my opinion as a rational human.

I have been trying to get an opportunity to send you $80.00, but it seems that I can't. So I will send you $20.00 in this letter. I will not risk more than that. I sent you 10 dollars in a letter not long since. I sent you ten more in a letter some 3 weeks ago.

My health is good. My love to all the family.

Your most affectionate son,

H. C. Kendrick.

N.B. You will please write to me as soon as you get this letter. Let me know whether you get the money or not.

Yours   S.C.

H.C.

LETTER 33 REPLY

Dear H.C.

After I walked out of my high school and before my father obtained my diploma, I was in a precarious position. Without a high school degree, I could not get into a college. And, if I was not going to college, on the day I turned 18, I was eligible for the draft during the Vietnam War.

So, on my 18th birthday, I did my duty. I registered for the draft so my nation could force me to help them defeat the evil communists. The U.S. military then loaded me onto a bus with dozens of others and drove us to Richmond for a day of physical and mental tests to make sure that we had what it took to defeat evil communism.

It was a real mess.

I did not want to do it.

I was pissed off.

I then returned home and figured it was only a matter of time before my number was pulled in the draft lottery. But, unlike you, I was not itching for a fight. I was not itching for battle.

I was certain I'd soon be sent off to die in a war that I did not support.

I was mad.

I hadn't really lived to that point. I hadn't even been with a woman yet. I was a virgin.

I wanted to see the country and experience true freedom before I was drafted.

So, that's what I did.

I'd saved quite a bit of money to that point, so rolled $900 in cash into my shoe, packed a few changes of clothes and a blanket in a backpack, and I was off, without telling my parents that I was leaving, let alone would be gone for only God knew how long.

I hitchhiked all the way to South Carolina by my first nightfall and then hiked into the woods to sleep under a tree. It was exhilarating to have no plan.

I met all sorts of people over the next few months– crooks, hobos, hippies. I met a man who claimed to be a murderer. I hung out with motorcycle gangs. I took rides from nice people and creepy people. I had gay men offer me money for sex, which I declined, but I did lose my virginity to a woman.

I grew my hair long and became a street person. I wasn't homeless. Nor was I a hobo. I had money and didn't need a job or to beg. I was just living a simple life. Most importantly – I was living.

People were always messing with me, which made me regret how I messed with the hobos when I was a kid. Someone would offer me a ride but then screech off just as I was reaching for the door handle or toss trash out the window at me and then drive off.

I learned how to get free hotel showers. When cleaning a motel in the morning, the crew foreman would unlock the doors to every vacant room for the crew. I could then slip into one for a shower and then out before I was noticed.

A young couple, along the way South, in Atlanta offered to take me all the way to Orlando, Florida where I slept in the bushes just outside downtown.

Orlando was where I first found trouble. There was a Morrison's Café. I went in, ate, and then decided not to pay. I could afford the meal but wanted to be a bad ass and walk out. It was stupid. The manager ran after and caught up to me. He called the police. I paid for the meal at the police station which was more expensive than at the cafeteria. Not a good financial decision.

I should have realized that I was pressing my luck, but I didn't.

I left Orlando for Atlanta, Georgia. In Atlanta, I discovered an abandoned home slated for demolition, so I slept on the floor for a few days.

A few days later, I took some drugs that a stranger offered me. Smart move.

The drugs kicked in while I was at a restaurant. Too stoned to control myself, I vomited inside the establishment and then stumbled outside.

The next thing I knew, I was being arrested. I needed to get to the hospital, but the three police officers instead clamped the handcuffs so tightly on me that my circulation was cut off. I yelled something. I don't remember what, but it was probably stupid. The police replied by jacking up my arms all the way to the back of my head. To alleviate the pain, I started jumping up and down, because doing so brought my arms back down. That's when one cop hit me in the chest and another across the face as hard as they could. From there, it just escalated, and I woke up hours later in a downtown jail cell.

In less than a year I had transitioned from a respectable young man training to be a restaurant manager into a long-haired hippie at war with the establishment. A rebel!

But not like you, a really despicable one.

Many despised me, including myself!

I'm tired. You will have to excuse me.

There is still much more to this story. I will finish it in my next letter.

Yours,

Ben

LETTER 34

Camp near Fredericksburg, Va.
Feb. 9th, 1863

Dear parents & family;
Your very highly appreciated letter sent by W. Morse, reached me on yesterday, - was received with gladness, an perused with great interest, though, the box you sent me, of which it gave account was lost. I regret very much, the loss of my box. I heard of it before William Morse got to the company. You know, I was proud to hear of it. I expected to get a good bite out of it, But alas! It was lost.

The way it got lost, was this: On the way from Wilmington, N.C. to Weldon, N.C., about 15 miles south of the latter place, the car in which my box was, broke loose from the train. This, not having been found out by the men in charge, it was left there until they got to Weldon; when William Morse went back to get them, my box was gone. So I was sadly disappointed.

Parents, I feel under as many obligations to you for sending it, as if I had enjoyed the contents thereof. I would rather, you would not send me any more boxes, unless a man is sent to Ga. for the expressed purpose of bringing them. I know it is quite a pleasure to you to send, and it is no less pleasure to me to receive, but our momentary physical enjoyments should not transcend the bounds of frugality. I know it costs more trouble to you than it is worth to me. Don't think my obligation to you, to be small, for it is to the contrary.

I was glad to hear that you got the money I sent to you. I will send you $40.00 more as soon as I draw again. I sent $20.00 in a letter long since. I keep as much as $50.00 in hand all the time, in case I should get sick.

It is with great difficulty, I write any thing of interest. The military is very dull, but indications are good however for active military operations shortly.

General Joseph Hooker[1] is now commander-in-chief of the yankee army of the Potomac, and says he intends to fight the rebels where he can find them. I am inclined to think, he will be met with effect where he makes the attempt. The idea prevails with the yanks, that general Longstreet[2] has gone down to Tenn. to take charge of the army commanded by gen. Braxton Bragg, but if they will come over the Rappahannock river, they will, I think, find Longstreet to their sorrow.

We sometimes, have a hint of peace given as in the Richmond papers, while this of course, naturally spiritualizes, cheers, and in a great measure, defines the perceptions of the thoughts and emotions of the Southern Soldier, he is no less actively engaged, making such preparations as would insure to him safety should an advance be made by the enemy.

2 men from our company have gone home on furlough. I don't have any idea, I will be at home any more before the war closes, though I would enjoy a trip home now very much indeed. It is strange a soldier wants to go home, when he has been from home so long and become addicted to camp life! But notwithstanding, the many vices and immoralities to which he is subject, and though he willingly goes on the battle field, and thereby is made to stand the whistling of the bullets, and the bursting of the bombs; and beholds the battle field with all its frightful carnage; when he gets to his quarters of rest and repose, he finds in him a refined principle which recurs with much anxiety to the once enjoyed pleasures of home.

I got a letter from brother Thommie some days ago, which stated, he was well. And one from brother Joseph. He was well, had stood the camp life, much better than he expected. 3 days ago, I was with cousins, - Daniel, Bennie, and Sammie Kendrick all day long. They came over to see me, they are in our division.

---

1   Defeated in the battle of Chancellorsville that occurred from April 30 – May 6, 1863, he resigned his post in November 1863.

2   James Longstreet. He was Gen. Robert E. Lee's second-in-command.

Please excuse me for not writing to you all separately, for I have some other correspondents.

In bringing the boxes I started to Va., with I left them in Richmond, because I could not get them farther. They stayed there, until a few days ago, when they, or that is the portion was left, were sent to me. Sergt. J. B. McCrary brought them to me. I sold what few there were, and sent the money to Mrs. Powell by Bateman.

Some of Cole Buchanan's cloths were left. They were stollen and Waldrop's also. I am very sorry for Mrs. Waldrop indeed, as she needed the money. Tell Mr. Buchanan, when Cole was killed, he had $25 but Dr. Childs paid 5D³ to David Jameson whom Cole was owing.

My love to all the family. Write soon.

Your most affectionate son.

H. C. Kendrick.

PS. I like the cloth of which, you sent me a specimen. I think it will make beautiful dresses to wear even to church of a Sunday.

I am in the best health I ever was in my life. I weigh 182 lbs.; more, than any of your children ever weighed. If I had sense in proportion to my physical powers, I would be sharp indeed. I am well aware, that the physical man, as a general thing always sympathizes with the mental man, but I am one of the exceptions to this rule.

As ever yours,

H.C.K.

---

3   5D – written here as in letter and meaning $5.00.

LETTER 34 REPLY

Dear H.C.

I wasn't taken directly to a cell. First, the police stripped me down, found the money in my shoe and kept every last penny. They took the whole damn thing and laughed as they did. I hadn't done anything wrong other than thrown up in public. They had no right to arrest me, let alone treat me like that.

They weren't done. As they walked me cuffed into an elevator, they slammed my head into it repeatedly. Bam. Bam. Bam. They continued to mock me, laughing that I would never say a word about any of it because no one would believe me anyway. I was supposed to get one phone call under law. I was going to call my parents and beg them to come get me, tell them I was in over my head and that I needed their help. I needed my parents. But I didn't get that phone call.

I notice your letters were getting longer at this point. And you asked your family to write more. I can sense, like me, you missed your mom and dad. You needed them. Do not be embarrassed or ashamed. Do not feel less manly. I believe it is natural to want our mommy and daddy when things get tough, especially when we are most afraid.

I was left in that cell, in general population, beaten, bloodied, and with ripped clothes. Looking back, I was only in that cell for one reason – to heal. They did not want me back out in the world with a wound to show for my time there.

Each night, guards would come by and bring us some sort of slop that they called food. Each night, I asked for my call and when I would be going home. And, each night, they ignored my questions.

Besides those questions, I kept my mouth shut and my eyes down while there. There were 16 or 17 people in the cell, and too many of them were looking for trouble. I did not want them to find me.

The baddest man there had to be around 6'2" tall, and 275 pounds of muscle rippling from his skin. He had a smaller guy, probably half his size, who did his bidding. If he wanted a cigarette from a certain guy, he sent his minion. If the man would not give up a cigarette, the minion backed away to make room for the boss. That's when it got ugly.

About halfway into my time there, a marine joined us in the cell. I don't know what he did, if he did anything at all to anger that bad man and deserve his wrath. He tore that marine from bed in the middle of the night and beat his head so badly against the cell bars that it swelled to the size of a small watermelon.

The next day, the military police came to get the marine. They didn't flinch or seem to care in the least when they saw his condition. They picked him up and forced him to walk, cuffed, from the cell with them.

Perhaps a week later, after what seemed to be an eternity in that hell, I was healed, released, and went home.

I recall the story of your father the first time he returned home to see his mother in Talbot County. It had been five months since he'd left home to venture out on his own and seek his fortune. When your grandmother gazed upon him for the first time, she wept, "My boy, my boy," and embraced him as the two continued to weep for joy.

I did not get the same reception.

I wanted to rush into the house and tell my parents everything, and not just about the trip, but everything.

But, instead, I walked into the house after many months away, said some standard hellos, and that was it. They never asked where I'd gone, and I never told them.

As for the draft lottery, luckily, I was never called.

Your loving nephew,

Ben

LETTER 35

[*February 22, 1863*][1]
Camp near Richmond Va.

Dear father:

The portion of the army to which I belong, having moved some considerable distance from the place at which I wrote my last letter to you, I feel it to be a duty devolving upon me as a son, to inform you of my whereabouts.

I will in the first place give you a brief sketch of my move.

On the 17th of this month, we got orders from head quarters, to get ready to move by day light the next morning; to pack all surplus baggage, and send it to the railroad to be put on the cars.

Having done this, we, knowing we would have to rise early next morning, lay down to sleep. Next morning, we were aroused by the peal of the drum, one hour before day.

When we arose, we found the ground covered with white, but unpleasant snow. The military, knowing nothing of shrinking from inclement weather, we of course, were actively engaged in making such provisions, as would insure to us comfort on the march, should the bad weather continue.

At the appointed hour, we were in line, and marched off.

The weather continued inclement - snowing very rapidly, and we knew nothing of our destination. But the presumption was with us, that our generals knew what they were doing, and would do that they thought best for our country consequently, marched on without a murmur.

It snowed all day the first day we marched. The night of the first day, was much suffering among the troops. Having been sick all day, that night, my good Capt. gave me permission to visit a neighboring house to shelter my-self from the bad weather, some 400 yards from the camp of the night. - I thanked him, and left for the house.

---

1   Author has inserted this date based on date written on archived letter.

The next morning about day, I came back to the company, - felt very well, at least, enough so to make the march. So, we started.

It began to rain in a few moments after we started from the camp, rained all day long prodigiously, and it was bitter cold. On that night, it rained also, which rendered us very uncomfortable indeed. Feeling that night, very well, I would not presume to ask a favor above that of the camp.

Now, comes the 3rd day. Having rained so much the night and day previous, the snow had all disappeared. This was of no great advantage to our marching, as the mud was very deep, from 6 to 12 inches. Having been prompted by every thing good, great, and noble, we split the mud like war horses. But the night of the 3rd day found us within 7 miles of Richmond.

The fourth day, we had very good road. So, we marched with apparently, little difficulty. The night of the fourth day, we got to this camp. We lay down that night, and in less than half an hour after we lay down, it began to snow rapidly. The next morning, we couldn't find each other, only as we would see the snow move where he was.

I don't know Pa, where we will go from here. We are just here awaiting orders from the higher military authorities. I had as soon believe, we will go down south when we leave here as north, east, or west. I think the enemy will abandon the idea of taking Richmond as they have tried so often in vain. They will make demonstrations elsewhere, perhaps, at Charleston S.C., Vicksburg Mississippi and Savannah Georgia.

My health is good. Write soon.

In two miles of Richmond on the south side.

Your son.

H. C. Kendrick

LETTER 35 REPLY

Dear H.C.,

I have friends who are married who could not have children.

That's not so unusual.

There are plenty of people whom, for a variety of genetic and health reasons, cannot have children. But how these friends went about having children did not seem normal to me at the time. They could have adopted, but they went a different route to ensure that they could tell people that a child was biological kin.

They went to South America, where they had a deal with a pregnant teen. Once she gave birth, the doctor would sign the birth certificate (for a fee) that my friends were the biological parents because he delivered the baby. My friends then went to the embassy to announce that the wife had given birth while they were there on vacation. The child was declared an American Citizen-born abroad, and they returned to raise the baby as their biological child. I think the entire ordeal cost them $10,000. I later learned that is a common way to smuggle a baby into the United States.

I lied to you.

Or perhaps it is better to write that I did not tell you the entire story.

In an earlier letter, I detailed the mystery of my son's birth.

The truth is that it is not a mystery, to me at least.

I don't know why I left out the details. Perhaps I did so to protect others. Perhaps it is because while I believe I know the truth, I also acknowledge that I lack evidence and could be wrong.

It is strange as a soldier wants to go home, when he has been from home so long and become addicted to camp life! But notwithstanding, the many vices and immoralities to which he is subject, and he willingly goes on the battlefield, and thereby is made to stand the whistling of the bullets, and the bursting of the bombs; and beholds the battlefield with all its frightful carnage; when he gets to his quarters of rest and repose, he finds in him a refined principle which recurs with much anxiety to the once enjoyed pleasures of home.

If you were brave enough to mentally survive such war, I should be able to finish my story. But I will do so cautiously so as to protect the identities of some. I do not know why I feel the need to do so, especially when writing to a ghost, but I do.

I believe I know the identity of my son's biological father and I know the identity of his biological mother, who was not my ex-wife.

Here is my theory:

My then-wife invited an adult male relative from South America to stay with us in Arlington while he adjusted to a new life here in the United States. At that same time, a 12-year-old female relative was also staying with us.

At some point before, my wife concocted the story of the inheritance and her own pregnancy. When the 12-year-old was sent to South America, I think that girl was pregnant.

I think my wife, for whatever reason, had the doctor sign the birth certificate declaring that the son was hers and mine.

During our divorce, on the record, I stated my theory and asked for a DNA test from the two whom I suspected to be the biological parents, but they refused.

Why would they refuse unless I was right?

I fought hard for that DNA test and for them to admit the truth.

I eventually gave up, realizing it was not worth the effort.

What would change?

He would still be MY son, regardless.

As I stated earlier, none of this changed my relationship with my son. He is my son. PERIOD. And I am glad that my ex-wife did what she did.

During one of my trips to Central America, while I was waiting at an intercity bus station, I couldn't finish a soda that I was drinking from a paper cup. So, I was looking for a trash can, which is a dead giveaway that I am not from there. (trash was indiscriminately thrown on the ground) A young woman who witnessed what she likely considered to be a pending wasteful act grabbed the cup from my hand and began feeding the soda to her baby in a blanket cradled in her arms. It struck me as odd. She didn't know who I was. She didn't know if I was sick. I could have infected her baby with something awful.

It got stranger.

She told me that she knew I was an American. I had no idea how. Perhaps it was my clothes. I replied with a nod that she was correct. She then tried to hand me her other child who was standing by her side, a little girl perhaps 4 years old with pretty green eyes, begging me to take her little girl back with me and to raise her as my own daughter. Again, she didn't know me. I could have been a drug dealer, pimp, or child trafficker. I might have only intended to harm her daughter. Yet, she was willing to take that chance because she had so little and knew her daughter would have so little too. My son could have ended up in such a situation. Instead, he ended up with me and today is a doctor. It's funny how life is.

As for my son's biological mother, she turned out fine too. I did track down her father though. I felt someone had to tell him what had happened to his daughter. He said he didn't believe me. He implied that I could not be right because a girl of 12 cannot have a baby.

I think that he believed me. It was just easier to deny the truth.

That's human nature, I guess.

As ever yours,

Ben

LETTER 36

Dear brother:

Yours of the 13th inst.[1] came to hand on yesterday, - was gladly received and with interest perused. I was glad to learn you were at Savannah Ga. again.

On the 17th of this month, we got orders to get ready to move by daylight the next morning; to send off all surplus baggage to the depot, and have it put on the cars. Having done this, we lay down to sleep. Knowing, we would have to get up the next morning by day, if not before. So, the next morning about 1 hour and a half before day, we were aroused by the peal of the drum.

When we got up, we found the ground white with snow and it still snowing rapidly. But as the military knows nothing of shrinking from inclement weather, we of course, were no less actively engaged in making all such preparations as would insure to them comfort in case the bad weather should continue.

The first day, it snowed all day which produced great consternation among the pedestrian soldiers, yes, even among horsemen. On the night of the first day, there was great suffering among the soldiers; the snow having been 10 or 12 inches deep. I having been a little sick, my Capt. granted me permission to stay at a neighboring house about 400 yards distant from the camp of that night.

Now comes the 2nd day. 1 hour before day, it began to rain - rained most prodigiously all day, and it was bitter cold. With great difficulty, we marched the 2nd day. At night, the rain was still falling in great haste. Having felt very well that night, I would not presume to ask a favor above that of the

---

1   Inst. meaning "present, current". Is used with a date to indicate the current month. (The Library, Springfield, Missouri, Abbreviations in Genealogical Research, pub. January 27, 2009, Renee)

camp. So, I stayed with the boys. I was wet all night but did not suffer a great deal from cold.

The 3rd day, it's having rained so much, the snow all disappeared, which was of no particular advantage to us, the mud having been from 6 to 14 inches deep. The weather was cold and forbidding, but we kept from suffering by physical exertion. The 3D day, we marched within 7 miles of Richmond.

On the fourth day, we had a pleasant time, the road having gotten much better. As we got closer to Richmond the road got more sandy, consequently, was much better. The 4th day, we got to the camp at which we are at now. We are within 2 ½ miles of Richmond, on the South side of James River. We are here awaiting orders. I think the yanks will dispense with the idea of taking Richmond.

I think they will [put] an effort elsewhere, perhaps at Charleston S.C., Vicksburg Mississippi and Savannah Ga.

I would not be surprised to be sent at any point even down South.

Our camp is not very pleasant, as we have nothing but pine wood to burn, which you know I hate more especially green.

You and brother Joe, will receive this letter for both.

I got a very nice Valentine the other day, I have no idea, however, who sent it to me.

My health is good. I weigh 182 lbs.

My love to my relatives in that co.

As ever, your loving brother,

H. C. Kendrick

N.B. brother, I don't know that I will get a transfer to your comp.[2] As I would sacrifice too much by doing it. I know, you would not have me sacrifice any comfort to get me in your comp. I will perhaps get to see you before long in moving over the country.

As ever yours, S.C.

H.C.K.

---

2   Company abbreviated.

LETTER 36 REPLY

Dear H.C.,

For a spell, I was a labor union organizer in Tampa.

I was a member of the carpenters' union and have long believed that labor unions are a backbone of the American workforce. We ensure that all workers are treated fairly.

My job as an organizer included doing undercover work on non-union jobsites to recruit prospective union members to sign authorization cards and to call for an election in order to turn a nonunion job into a union one. It's what we called "salting" a job.

There was the time, for instance, that a local power plant was to be constructed by a firm that was non-union and would purposely not hire union workers because doing so meant the site had to live up to certain pay, safety and health protocols demanded by the union.

As a "salt", I applied for a job on one of the company's other worksite's as though I was not a member of the union. Once hired, I quietly sought to recruit others to join by preaching the benefits and having workers sign authorization cards. If enough workers joined the union, the job would become regulated by the union, providing better pay and conditions.

The job's project manager learned what I was doing and fired me. He gave me the excuse that they were over budget and had to let people go. He even turned his pockets inside out to accentuate the situation.

I called his BS and said that we all knew I was being let go for one reason and that was because I was union. I'd done a good enough job of recruitment that other workers went to bat for me.

I filed a complaint with the National Labor Relations Board, accusing the construction company of firing me because I was union. They ruled in my favor.

The contractor remained in charge of the power plant job but was just a figure-head. The project was forced to hire union workers and a large union contractor basically took over as head of the job. By the way, the project was in the cost range of a half billion dollars and that was in the early 1980's.

Your captain reminds me of a union organizer. He understood that it was important to look out for the health of his men when possible. He wanted to make sure you were healthy and well. What good could you have done later in battle if you were weak? You would have added to the number of soldiers but added little to the fight. Your captain would have been simply sending you to be slaughtered.

It was the same with the union. We looked out for the safety and wellbeing of our members. Someone must. Sometimes, a company cares more about their bottom line than the safety of their employees.

I was not always successful in turning a jobsite union.

On another occasion, I was sent to unionize the construction of a downtown Tampa parking garage. I did as I always did. I applied as though I was nonunion and then sold the benefits of being union to the other workers. During breaks, I passed authorization cards to the nonunion workers, all they had to do was sign it and then a vote would transpire through the National Labor Relations Board.

I knew that would be a tough site to unionize. All of its foremen and superintendents were disgruntled former union guys. They were not just against the unions; they hated the labor organizations due to personal disagreements they'd previously had with union management.

A few days into that job, the carpentry superintendent pulled me aside. He was blunt. If I'd told them upfront that I was union, they'd have made me a boss and paid me a nice wage to keep my mouth shut. Instead, I'd gone behind their backs, he said, and if I did not immediately cease what I was doing, I could end up in a ditch on the side of the road like the last union rep who tried to pull off what I was attempting. He even provided the victim's name. Perhaps the boss was bluffing about their involvement. But maybe he was not. So, I backed off that job.

I love the union but not enough to die for it.

I was seeking to better the lives of others.

That company was so against improving their employees' lives that they were willing to hurt someone. That company is not an anomaly. Other companies believe their bottom line comes first and the safety of others is second.

Governments sometimes believe that too. Our government has long believed that unions are a danger to governments. Better working conditions are not only the responsibility of the companies. The government plays a role too.

Unions lobby governments for worker rights and vote in blocks for those who support them. But some powers-that-be believe that worker rights infringe upon their rights. Better pay and better working conditions mean less money in their already hefty bank accounts.

So, governments have been known to infiltrate unions on local, state, national, and international levels. Sometimes they do so obviously. When the railway union went on strike in the 1890s and blocked trains from traveling, they did so for better pay and working conditions. The federal government sent in troops to successfully squash the strikes.

Other times, it is done quietly.

In the 1970s, Australian labor unions opposed the United States using their nation as a base for defense facilities. So, the CIA infiltrated those unions to sow distrust and get what they wanted.

Also in the 1970s, the CIA financed labor union strikes in Chile to disrupt the economy so as to inspire a coup to overthrow a leader of whom they did not approve.

Unions should be powerful tools for bettering society. They should not be weaponized.

I will write again soon.

As ever, yours loving nephew,

Ben

LETTER 37

Dear mother & father:

I don't know whether I can answer your letters of the 4th acceptably or not, as I have written to sister Nancy. I was glad to get a line from home. I had rather hear from home than any where else. But yet, it seems like I get letters from home more seldomly, than any where else. I am perfectly satisfied, however, that I am not for one moment forgotten; still, I don't get as many letters from home as I write, I have nothing of interest to write as the movements of both parties are so dull and inactive. When we are still, I can't get any news of any importance to write. You perhaps, have received the letter I wrote you, giving a sketch of my trip from Fredericksburg to Richmond.

Mother, I don't know how to express my gratitude to you and Sis. Bettie for sending me clothing, or rather preparing them for me. The gratitude with which my heart swells, is of that nature which characterizes alone, strict obedience and motherly love. Mother, my language would only be expressive of idleness, were I to presume to say, that I will ever be able to indemnify you either by a close observance of maternal respect, or by evidencing in my daily deportment a never dying gratitude for a mother's care.

Father, how are you getting along with the farm? I guess you are more closely confined than agrees with your age. Great God! Hasten the day when parents and children may again unite together, that that, for which we were created, may be accomplished; that parents may be comforted by their children, and that children may receive from their parents such instructions as may ever impress their minds with the important duty of filial love to God and becoming obedience to parents.

Father, I feel the importance of prayer, and the need of it. I haven't a doubt but that my case is presented to the care of God daily and hourly. I feel that there will be no such a thing as peace until the hearts of the citizens and soldiers, get right and become humble before God. We must be soldiers of the cross, as well as of the confederate fields.

We have meeting nightly in this regt. which no doubt, is doing great good. When you get this, write me where brother R.S. is, and what he is doing, that he doesn't write to me. With this, I close.

My love to the family and inquiring friends.

Your devoted son,

H. C. Kendrick

P.S. I wrote Sister E. a letter yesterday, not having any idea I would get a letter today. I expect she will think it rather cutting, but tell her to parden me.

Where is aunt Sarah Trussell? It seems she is not mindful of me.

Tell Johnie and Bennie to write to me. They are getting large enough to write me. It will be of no disadvantage to them, but a considerable advantage. Write me Bennie & Johnnie.

Yours, [t.c.]

H.C.K.

LETTER 37 REPLY

Dear H.C.,

My parents did not attend church on a regular basis, thus I did not either.

That alienated me as a kid from the rest of the neighborhood that did attend church regularly.

So, when I was around 6 or 7, I asked my parents if I could check out the local Methodist Church where my friend's father was the pastor. They did not want to take me, but dressed me in my Sunday best and sent me on my way, on my own.

I applaud your regiment's devotion to prayer, the Bible, and the word of God.

I must believe that faith and not artillery was your greatest ally in the struggle.

Guns will slay your enemies, but faith might help you through the hard emotional times when you are lonely, cold, bored, or afraid.

You likely inherited your faith from your father, who helped and then served as deacon at Talbot County's first church.

As the family story goes, your father's congregation initially met at parishioner homes. They needed a church building, but there was debate whether that was the best use of early resources when some residents were still without lodging and the county needed more farms.

But then one resident at a meeting made a convincing argument in favor of one.

"Men and brethren," he said. *"we know every word that has been spoken is the truth and we know that man's responsibility begins with his home. But, brothers, we also know we have a bigger responsibility toward our God and have pledged ourselves for the*

furthering of his kingdom. How do we know how many souls may perish if we do not open a door to them? Yes, brothers, we have heavy responsibilities, but I for one, am not willing to thrust any aside. By God's help, I expect to meet both. Right now, I am in the midst of building against the cold winter and so are you, but let's each of us give one day out of the six for building on the Lord's house and the seventh for worshipping in his holy temple."

Everyone supposedly left that meeting excited to build the church, but none were more excited than your father who drew up the plans before he fell asleep that night, led the construction and was later known to lead the congregation in song during services.

When I arrived at my first service, I was told children were not allowed to attend the actual service. Instead, along with all the children, I was ushered into a room for Sunday school where we learned the basics of the Bible.

I attended that class every Sunday for around three or four weeks. Then, one Sunday, the teacher handed out small Bibles with pictures to everyone in class except me. As I sat there, looking at the teacher with eyes asking why I had been skipped, she addressed the entire class. Ben would not be receiving a Bible, she said, because my parents did not go to church.

It hurt.

When class was over, I walked home and never went back.

Because of this experience, religion has never played a major part in my life, if a part of it at all. It's bizarre how much a childhood experience can shape us if we allow it.

Your nephew,

Ben

LETTER 38

Camp near Richmond Va.
March 9th, 1863

Dear Sister;

I received your kind letter of the 4ᵗʰ inst. not more than 20 minutes ago - was glad to hear from home once more. I had almost [despaired] of ever getting a letter from you again; as I got letters from all my correspondences but from those at home. Don't think me in the least tired of writing to you; for it is with a pleasure not to be expressed by an ordinary mind, that I write to my dear friends, not only friends, but relatives at home.

Sis., you talked of having visited the Dr. since I left. I was glad to hear he was doing well, and in good health.

The times are very dull at this time in camp. It is with the greatest difficulty imaginable, that I can write a letter at all whether interesting or not. I have nothing much to do, as the military is extremely dull and inactive. All I do is, eat, sleep, and walk over camps. We are as near the point of do nothing, as we have ever been since we have been in the service. It seems, that stillness pervades our camp. We are excited only when the cars pass bearing citizens, by whom we are reminded of those loved ones at home.

Sis., I went over to the 15th Alabama Regt., and saw cousins Bennie, Samie, and Daniel Kendrick. They send their love to all the family. I also saw Wash. Bass an old schoolmate of mine, he is a lieutenant in his company, was elected a few days ago.

Sis.,, we have an association in the brigade called the Soldiers Christian Association of the 3D Brigade, Hood's division, first army Corps. I have not joined it however, as I perhaps could not attend regularly. I attend it as regularly as I can. We have prayer meeting every night. I believe the power of God is getting in our regt., I feel that the boys are generally inclined to visit the meetings of the regt. There are some companies, nearly all of whom have joined this association.

Tell the Dr., I would appreciate a letter from him very much indeed.

My love to little H.. tell him I will write him a little letter. Do you suppose he recollects any thing about me?

Sis, I will close. My love to the family. Write me soon.

Your brother,

H. C. Kendrick

LETTER 38 REPLY

Dear H.C.,

Late in my mother's life, probably a year or two before she died in 2015, my girlfriend and I would take her out to lunch or dinner every Sunday afternoon.

As I have often written, my father was an open book about his life, but my mother was an abstract painting. She never spoke much about her past. She'd provide vague details here and there and I'd have to come up with my own meaning.

But she became more talkative during those lunches, often enjoying telling us about some of the famous people she'd met over the years. Whenever she did, the story would begin with her saying, "Did I ever tell you that I know so and so?" But she never really knew that person. It was just someone she met in passing.

For instance, my mother said she knew Jackie Kennedy, before she was our First Lady and wife to President John F. Kennedy. Jackie was a newspaper writer/photographer before meeting and marrying the future young, charismatic man who would become our President. She was covering a story that included my mother and snapped a picture of her. That was it. That was the extent of their relationship, but, to my mother, that meant they knew one another.

It was endearing and something I loved about her.

But it also misled me on one occasion.

Hasten the day when parents and children may again unite together. That that for which we were created, may be accomplished; that parents may be comforted by their children, and that children may receive from their parents such instructions as may ever impress their minds with the im-

portant duty of filial love to God and becoming obedience
to parents.

In a way, those lunches were a reunion with my mother. We were
perhaps closest during that time than we'd been since I was a child,
perhaps ever.

During one of those Sunday lunches with my mother, my girlfriend and I mentioned that we had just watched Schindler's List, a
movie about the Holocaust and Nazi Germany.

And my mother responded with one of her, "Did I ever tell you I
know so and so" stories. She mentioned, almost in passing, that she
worked with a Nazi while she was at the David Taylor Model Basin.
She didn't say more, and I didn't ask for more, figuring the man
perhaps lived in Germany during the war, came to the United States
and then visited the Model Basin as a delivery man or something.

If I had known then what I know now, I would have asked questions. If I had known that she really did know a Nazi, as in she
REALLY did know one personally, well, I would have continued
the conversation. But why would I have suspected anything? How
was I to know?

So, the topic was dropped, and I did not think of it again until a
few years later after her passing. The moments that fleet before us
to be embraced, yet we do not see to grasp them and hold on, if only
for that moment.

Yours,

Ben

P.S. Chris, The young charismatic President Kennedy was
assassinated in broad daylight November 22 1963, while being
filmed. The only suspect was gunned down in public 2 days after, and
5 days later The Warren Commission was established to investigate
the President's Assassination. One of the 7 men on the commission
was Allen Dulles, Former C.I.A. Director, who resigned in 1961
under pressure over political differences with the president. Even
today, after 50 years, rumors persist today of C.I.A. complicity in
President Kennedy's Murder. The cursory Warren investigation
concluded that no conspiracy transpired.

Which side does *the power of God* favor?

LETTER 39

Camp near Richmond, Va.
March 22nd, 1863

Dear father and mother,

I received your letters together with the clothing you sent me by L. I. Fuller a few days ago, was glad to hear from you, and feel thankful to you for the clothing you sent me. You may be surprised, that I have not acknowledged the reception of the clothes and letters before now, by writing; but it was entirely out of my power to do so sooner than I am.

The morning after I got the clothes, 1 hour before day, orders came in great haste to move. We get ready to move, and moved 1 ½ or 2 miles from camp in the direction of Richmond, when we were stopped - , General Hood called us all around him, and told us what we might depend upon.

Says General Hood, "Gentlemen, Soldiers, and officers, I have not called you up this morning for the purpose of making a speech, for I haven't the time. But I wish to inform you what you have to do; you will not be surprised if you have to march hard, perhaps harder than ever before. I suppose many of you have left camp this morning without your breakfast, and I am here without sleep on account of the order. We are going to meet the enemy, and I want my division to be behind none in contending with those yankee scoundrels."

Those were the words of General Hood.

We marched in the direction of Fredericksburg, 22 miles that day. Soon after we stopped, General Hood received orders not to move farther in that direction until further orders, as Early's Brigade[1] had driven the enemy back. We remained there one day. Late in the evening, it began to snow with a fair prospect of a continuation for a day or two. It snowed all night and was still snowing the next morning.

We started that morning about 7 o,clock back toward Richmond, which place we reached 3 o'clock in the evening,

---

1   Led by Major General Jubal A. Early who led the Army of Northern Virginia.

snowing rapidly all day. It seems every time we start to Fredericksburg, it rains or snows one. You at once perceive we must have been very tired when we reached camp, having marched 22 miles through snow, in 8 hours. We were glad when we heard the order to go back to Richmond. I am truly tired of this cold weather; I would freely welcome pleasant weather, though I know it would bring about the most active military operations.

You can perhaps imagine the feelings of the soldier when he marched up to his camp, finding every thing covered with snow. And the soldier tired down with fatigue, and shivering with cold. I never saw every thing look so cold in my life. But we are well fixed up again.

I and my mess are the most fortunate beings in the world surely. It doesn't make any difference how gloomy the prospects may seem to be for comfort, we are sure to make ourselves comfortable by some means.

We will perhaps stay here some time, as the weather is very inclement. Nothing but a pashion of love for Southern destruction would move the yanks in the direction of Southern camps, all prudence would forbear to move at all at present.

I don't know that I have any thing more of interest to write you.

My love to all the family. Write soon. My health is good.

Your true son,

H. C. Kendrick.

P.S. father, when you write to cousin Bennie, Samie & Daniel, you will consign your letters to company (B.) 15th Ala. Regt. in care of Capt. Fagans.[2]

---

2   Captain Isaac B. Feagin, who commanded the Alabama 15th Infantry Regiment. The 15th Alabama is most famous for being the regiment that confronted the 20th Maine on Little Round Top during the Battle of Gettysburg on July 2, 1863. He was captured and spent 11 months in Federal Prison - he was exchanged in June 1864. He resigned or retired in December 1864. After the war he was elected sheriff of Barbour County in 1866. Died May 2, 1900, age 67. (Wikipedia) (antietam.atow.org)

LETTER 39 REPLY

Dear H.C.,

One of my closest friends had an older brother who played professional football. His brother, who has since passed, was going through rough times health-wise, and my friend was assisting his brother as best he could.

My friend and I were sitting in my office, and it was my turn to listen. He told me about how his brother was having difficulty with his reasoning skill and since he lived alone no one could help him. One day, for example, he saw a car in front of his house and walked out to confront the man in the car, words were exchanged and then the brother grabbed the man. Eventually the police arrived and consequently his brother was arrested. I mentioned that maybe the problems stemmed from his time as a football player. He explained that that didn't help, and the N.F.L. had sent him a check as a settlement, but the damage was probably caused when he was a child.

"In an odd way, my brother could thank our father for that," he replied.

Their father, it turned out, was a World War II combat veteran who returned and had to deal with injuries suffered. Perhaps not just physical, but also mental. The father self-medicated himself with alcohol on his own prescribed schedule, which was often. After which he would challenge the older brother to fist fights. So, he'd beat on his own son. As the son grew older and could defend himself, those beatings turned into violent fistfights. Every Friday night, my friend told me, their father stumbled home drunk ready for another go around. "Of course," my friend explained to me, "my older brother became the toughest man I have ever known." My friend told me stories that day about the terrible life his brother lived at home as a boy, and how the abuse plagued him the rest of his life.

Through these letters, I detailed my abuse. But those details were lost for years, pushed into the recess of my brain, and replaced with stories of salted watermelon. My brain did that purposely. It was protecting me. I knew it happened but pretended it did not and sought to forget.

There is that PTSD again.

An odd thing happened after my friend told me that story of abuse. For the first time since childhood, I suddenly remembered everything about my abuse. I could see his face as clear as day. I could smell that basement. I could remember that weird name, "Duane Crockett," and the old woman in the rocking chair. I could feel the heat of that day that softened the asphalt. I could feel his gaze, hear his voice, and feel the fear from his threats.

I wrote earlier of my PTSD as though it was in my past, as though I moved forward and lived a pain free life despite what happened to me. As I read your last letter about the difficulties you were facing, I wondered how your fellow soldiers who survived were able to adjust to normal life after that. I wondered if the nightmares that they lived forever haunted their dreams. I wondered about their PTSD. I then realized it was PTSD that kept me safe. My friend's story triggered it, as writing these letters have. But that might be a good thing. I am finally, maybe, ready to work through this. No, I have been working through this. Thank you, Chris, for listening.

These personal stories I have told you have each been triggered by something I read in your letters – my trip to Central and South America, my time on Ascension Island, the hobo jungle, my childhood friends and jobs, upbringing, lack of spirituality, parents' sexuality. Most are not directly connected to my abuse, but are indirectly connected to it via my confusion, loneliness, distrust, and more, each of which is due in large part to my abuse. Each reminds me in some way of that day in the basement, the fallout, my search for answers.

When my friend and I parted ways that day, I could not stop thinking about his football player brother and how I felt about him. I didn't feel guilty. I felt jealous. He knew his abuser's identity. He was able to face him and crack him in the head. I wanted that opportunity. I wanted revenge. But first, I wanted to know why. Why the hell had that man done that to me? Why would anyone do that to anyone?

Writing to you. Telling my stories. This exercise. It has not been futile. If not for your help, I would not be ready to do what I am about to do in the coming letters. I will admit what I believe to be the truth, no matter how hard it is to do.

I now know you are with me. That was not just wind twirling about that day when I visited the place where you died. That was you. It's the only way to explain all of this. It's the only way to explain how these letters have helped me. I have not just been reading them. You have been reading them to me.

It's the only way to explain the timing.

> *But I wish to inform you what you have to do; you will not be surprised if you have to march hard, perhaps harder than ever before. I suppose many of you have left camp this morning without your breakfast, and I am here without sleep on account of the order. We are going to meet the enemy, and I want my division to be behind none in contending with those Yankee scoundrels.*

This realization comes at too coincidental of a time for it to be happenstance. The timing is too spot on. You planned it this way.

Your final letters detail your march into your final battle.

In a way, I too am now ready to march into battle.

H.C., let us march together.

Your true nephew,

Ben

LETTER 40

Dear father and family:

I received yours of the 18th inst. which afforded me a great pleasure indeed. I am at all times, and under all circumstance, glad to hear from home. I take desponding fits about nothing else, but not hearing from home. So you can easily imagine my desire to hear from you. As I have moved once since I wrote you, I deem it a duty devolving upon me to write you, which should not be neglected.

We are now at the camp we were at before, but came here after having made a very hard march. About 8 days ago, we received orders to get ready to leave camp. Having done this, we left in great haste, having marched 2 1/2 or 3 miles from camp in the direction of Richmond, we were halted, called up by General Hood, who told us what we had to do, and where we were going.

Says General Hood, "Gentleman, we are going to meet the enemy, and I want you to be at your post." But we did not get to the enemy, before we were turned back, and marched to camps near Richmond.

We are doing nothing now. The military is rather dull, but we are expecting to move in a short time; (that is,) we expect to change camps for the purpose of getting wood to burn. We are not expecting a great action of the military shortly, from the fact, that the weather is unfit for anything of that nature, the snow, however, has all disappeared. The ground is wet and disagreeable.

Father, you wanted me to give you the address of Cousins B.S. and D. Kendrick. Company (B) 15th Ala. Vols., Care of Captain Fagans.

I was with Cousin Ben yesterday; he told me Cousin Daniel was sick at the Chimborazo Hospital in Richmond. Ben said

Daniel would get a discharge, or at least make an effort to that effect. I think Cousin Sam had better get one too, as he is not able to march on account of his feet.

A.D. Chambless has gone to a hospital in Richmond to stay. He was detailed by a board of physicians.

I saw Wash Bass yesterday. He was well, and asked me all about you. He is a lieutenant in his company. Sam Fuller is not fit for the service of the field, and I guess he will get a detail of some kind, lighter than that of camp. He is not able to use a gun with his left hand. I hope he will get a clerkship of some kind (I.E.) for some quarter master, or commissary.

I received a letter from brother Thomas a few days ago. He was well. Brother Joseph was well too.

We have nothing to do, but sleep, eat and sit by our fires. We have a good chimney to our tent.

Father, perhaps you exert your-self too much for your strength. It is true, you have a great deal to do, but I would not exert my-self too much. Father, take care of your-self as well as possible, for without you I don't know what we will do. Consequently, I would advise you to save your-self, let all else go to destruction (I.E.) of a pecuniary nature.

I am satisfied, that without parents one is almost lost. My experience in this war, has long since taught me, that the worth of parents is inestimable. My parents look to your best interest, which consists in your self preservation.

My health is good. My love to all the family.

Your loving son,

Write me often.

H. C. Kendrick.

P.S. Bennie write every time father does for your improvement.

Mrs. Sarah Trussell; Dear aunt: Thinking it would be agreeable, I have reserved a small portion of my paper to write you a short letter. Aunt, you will please except my sincere thanks for the socks you sent me. I appreciate them very *highly indeed. Aunt, I hope you will be rewarded two fold at least. My heart is intensely enlisted in the interests of my relatives and friends at home. My category of news, is rather dull at present, as the military is dull and inactive. I don't expect we will have a great deal to do shortly, as the prospect for such a thing, is rather gloomy. Aunt, I will gladly receive a letter from you at any time.*

Tell Johnie to write to me.

As ever, your devoted Nephew.
H. C. Kendrick.

Brother Bennie:
I received the short letter you wrote me, at the time father wrote his, was glad to hear from you, but sorry to learn you had been sick. I hope [eve.]¹this reaches you, you will be able to resume your studies at school. Bennie, I want you to learn all you can, do your best. You know father loves to see his children do well. I want you to improve every moment you have. Devote your whole time to your books. Brother, you know every sentiment and emotion of my heart, is deeply concerned in the welfare of my brothers. Parden brevity.

Accept my love.

Good by your brother. Write me soon.
H. C. Kendrick.

---

1   Written eve. In letter; author is making a judgment it is an abbreviation for 'eventually'.

LETTER 40 REPLY

Dear H.C.,

Through my work in construction and real estate over the years, I'd become familiar with real estate records. When real estate changes hands, mortgages are made, and many other transactions are completed. A record is kept somewhere, such as the courthouse.

If you look deeply enough into a home or property's records, you can learn the full history, including every owner, sometimes referred to as the *chain of title*.

That hit me after that day with my friend. Perhaps, just as his brother faced his abuser, I could face mine. I could identify him through property records. Or at the very least, find who the property owner was at the time of the assault. I don't know why I never thought of that before. Hearing the story from my friend engaged me in the search.

That's not as easy as it sounds as this is not my occupation. I was able to do some work on the computer. I also hired a title search company to get copies of documents and go further in depth. Within weeks, he had the name of the family who owned the house where I was abused, at the time that I was abused! The same family had owned that house from 1940 through 1980.

They'd owned it for 40 years, yet I'd never heard that family name before. That didn't make any sense. We moved a lot, but always stayed within the same general area. That meant I got to know just about every family in that corner of Arlington County. I knew many people but yet, I had never heard the name of the family who'd owned a house up the street from me?

That could have meant only one thing. I rationalized, they had never lived there. They owned the home but rented it out and the person who abused me lived there for a short period, which is why it looked empty for so many years.

So, I needed to track down the former owner and ask for a list of their renters, I figured. Surely, they had records if they didn't recall all the names.

I started looking into the family.

Here is what I found:

> The patriarch bought the house in 1940 and died in the house 1953, leaving behind an elder widow.
>
> What's more, they also owned the house across the street.
>
> Wait, an old woman and a house across the street? A flash went off inside my head upon learning that information.
>
> I remembered the old woman in the rocking chair inside that house across the street. Was that the widow? Did she live across the street from her rental home where I was abused? If so, how could she have no idea what types of atrocities were going on there?
>
> Or was she drugged? She seemed drugged. The way she rocked and stared into space, she came off like a zombie, or someone who'd been lobotomized. Perhaps she never mentally recovered from the death of her husband and became depressed. Perhaps that explained how she could be unaware of what her tenant was up to.
>
> Census records showed she had two sons. Did they not know about the tenant? Did they not look into his past?
>
> Did they abandon their mother and leave that job up to her?
>
> Did they not help her with the rental home that likely paid her bills?

The only way to know was to ask them.

But I couldn't.

They were both dead. I found their obituaries.

Which in turn added more information that further clouded the situation.

The sons were my parents' age and they'd gone to George Washington University.

My father graduated from there. My mother took classes there. They weren't just my parents' age, they were peers. I wondered; did they know each other? Were they friends?

Also, according to their obituaries, they both worked for the CIA, one as an analyst and another as one of the tippy top men in the agency's personnel department.

I was floored by that revelation, specifically by the brother who worked in personnel.

Such a position meant he likely had to vet everyone who fell under his jurisdiction. He had to learn their every secret, every mistake. Remember, information is power. I was grilled by the federal government because I wanted to work a construction job in Russia. The federal government used to follow male and female employees as they went to bars to learn about their sexuality. Can you imagine the background checks for CIA employees? That brother who worked in personnel probably had the ability to learn what someone had for breakfast on a random Sunday five years ago. Yet, he wouldn't have looked into his family's tenant? And, if he had, he wouldn't have found any indication that the man was a monster? Wouldn't that concern him? Couldn't that have been used to extort him one day?

I had to learn more about that man.

His doctorate degree was in psychology, fitting for what I discovered a man in his position likely had to do. As I uncovered more about the CIA and their personnel department, I realized he was probably not solely in charge of those working directly for the federal agency. He likely also oversaw the programs that included those who indirectly worked for the CIA – the assets who worked as double agents, the drug dealers who fought their wars, those who headed shell companies funded by the CIA, and whose employees unknowingly supported secret government missions, and so on. That man had the capability at his fingertips to learn what was on your mind when you ate breakfast on a random Sunday five years ago. Yet, he had no idea that his family's tenant was a rapist?! He was ok with such a monster renting a home across the street from his mother?! IT. DID. NOT. MAKE. SENSE!

I dug deeper.

The son-of-a-bitch had a son. He had a son my age! He was either so ignorant that he put his son at risk of being raped during a visit to grandma, ceased having a relationship with his mother, or just did not care.

Wait, a son my age? Duane Crockett was my age. Could he have been?

I dug deeper.

I learned what high school he attended and found an Arlington library that had that school's old yearbooks. I found the man's photo. And I nearly blacked out.

It was my rapist.

It was him. That photo was him!

I had that image in my memory in case I ever met him again.

But, I can't even contain my emotions as I am writing.

I'd found the identity of my rapist!

I'd thought maybe solving the mystery would provide some closure.

I'd thought wrong.

I thought I'd learn my attacker was a drug addict, or a Satan worshipper, or some evil cultist and that would at least provide some explanation for why he did it.

But he was a high-ranking government official, husband, and father with an obituary singing his praises as a great man.

None of it made sense H.C.

So, I continued to dig.

And I continued to hate what I learned.

> *My experience in this war, has long since taught me, that the worth of parents is inestimable.*
>
> *My parents look to your best interest, which consists in your self-preservation.*

As ever, your devoted nephew,

Ben

LETTER 41

Dear father & family:

Your very kind letter of the 10th inst. reached yesterday, was glad to hear from you, and to hear you were well.

As we have moved some considerable distance from the place of my last letter, I guess you would like to learn where I am and what I am, and have been doing. I will commence by giving you a brief sketch of the march, and also a short history of the various movements at this point.

On the 8th of this month, we started from Petersburg to this point. We marched 5 days in succession, marched from 18 to 23 miles a day. As the evening of the 5th day, declined, we got very wearry. Consequently, we were halted in a piece of woods to rest as we thought, for the night, but shortly after we had pulled off our luggage and seated our wearied limbs to rest, we were ordered to move off in great haste 5 miles to the right, to prevent the enemy from pressing our right wing too hard. We went off in almost double-quick time to meet the yankee hessians, but when we got there, the enemy had declined coming. We stoped for the night.

The next day at early dawn we got intelligence, that the enemy had made a raid on our wagons in our rear about 15 miles. When we moved up there, we were nearly exhausted, scarcely able to move at all; but being prompted by every thing great, sacred, and noble, we moved off like men, like faithful soldiers.

When we got to our place of destination, we sent out a few scouts to reconnoitre the front to find out the enemy's force. When our scouts get to the enemy's cavelry, they (the enemy), ran like quarter-horses until they got out of our reach, when we pressed forward with our brigade, and followed them as fast as possible until we got within 600 yards of the pickets. When they began to fire on us at the rate of 50 times a minute.

We halted, having gone as far as we could in that direction. In a few minutes they began to throw shells at us from their gun-boats, bursting all around us, seem to threaten us with destruction. We had no protection at all, the ground having been perfectly level.

General Anderson sent to General Hood, that he did not like the position of his brigade. General Hood sent Anderson to leave that place. Shortly after we began to leave, the enemy discovered us leaving and began to run their canons upon us to enfilade our lines, to prevent this, we formed a line of battle to receive them, but they failed to come on us. Here, the brigade remained for the night, but our company with 3 others, were ordered to go down on the Nansemond River to put up breastworks.¹ We had to approach the river under cover of darkness, then expected to have a fine contest with a boat before we could get to the river's bank, but we met with no difficulty in approaching the river, no gun-boat having been near. I think we did this without the knowledge of the enemy.

We worked all night long without any sleep at all. Early the next morning, about twilight, the old gun-boat came up within 800 yards of our batteries when it stoped, and began to fire on our men. We did not return the fire at that time. The enemy's, seeing we would not fire on them, they moved up 200 yds. farther, when they cast anchor and began to fire again. Soon we opened on the boat with two parrot guns. The second fire from our guns, set the gun-boat on fire disabling it entirely. The crew managed to extinguish the fire, and two other boats were soon seen hitched to the large boat and towing it off. So they soon disappeared and made their appearance no more that day.²

1   On the upper Nansemond River, the Confederates constructed batteries at an old Confederate fort in the lower reaches of the Nansemond and nearer to Hampton Roads, Fort Huger (this became known as the 'Hill's Point Battery), and a second battery at a bend in the river just below Suffolk, near a local farm owned by the Norfleet family. This battery was known as the Norfleet House Battery.
2   H.C. describes in simple detail what he is seeing; and history remembers it as the USS Mount Washington became grounded and was crippled in the attack. The Hill's Point batteries also opened fire trapping Lamson›s flotilla

We remained there until the night of the next day, in the meantime, however, the enemy had erected 3 land batteries to play on our breastworks, and thereby, effect a passage for their gun-boats, but they failed in this operation. The weather was very inclement the next day, so much so, we all got very wet and cold. I and a good many others, Capt. Wellborn with us, went into an old barn near by to eat our breakfast of cracker and raw bacon. Capt Wellborn left there just before the yanks began to throw their missiles of destruction at the barn.

Soon after Capt. Wellborn left there, the enemy threw a shell at the barn, bursting near the barn, but hurting nothing. Finally, a well directed shell came sliping along to the barn striking it on the corner and the whole shell exploding in the barn, killing one man in Company H of our Regt. in 2 feet of me and two others badly wounded in about 4 feet of me; and I was considerably shocked a few grains of powder striking me in the face and knocking the skin from my cheek bone. So, I had no use for barns after that.

We are at rest in a piece of woods in 2 ½ miles of Suffolk. We go on picket once every 4 days. There is firing all the day on the picket line, sometimes wounding and sometimes killing some men on both sides. I think we will retreat from this place soon, as we have no position for fighting at this point.

I am in the best of spirits. My health is good.

My love to all the family and friends. Write me soon as you get this. You needn't be surprised if I should fail to write as often I have been writing, for the Summer Campaign[3] has opened.

Your son as ever.

H. C. Kendrick.

---

between them. As the tide rose the USS *Stepping Stones* helped free the Mount Washington.

3   H.C. calls it the Summer Campaign; history refers to this period of the Civil War as the Suffolk Campaign, Battle of Suffolk, or the Siege of Suffolk, commencing from April to May 1863. Engaged - 45,000. Union – 260 killed, wounded, missing. Confederate – 900 killed, wounded, missing.

LETTER 41 REPLY

Dear H.C.,

You wrote of the Yankees as though they were the ultimate bad guy.

You wrote of the Northerners as though they were pure evil.

H.C., not only were you misinformed and misled, but your generation was unable to imagine pure evil on a national scale. No one in the modern world could until the Nazis came along.

The modern world had never battled anything as evil as the Nazis, nor has since. They were not just content with killing and defeating their enemies, as is the norm in war. They wanted to torture their enemies and make them suffer. More than six million Jews died in the Nazi concentration camps in unimaginable ways – worked or starved to death, gassed, poisoned, suffocated, and even baked. There are stories of Nazi leaders making lamp shades out of skin of their prisoners.

And after we Americans helped vanquish the Nazis, we sought to adopt some of their methods.

I think we did this without the knowledge of the enemy.

The Nazis had been experimenting on prisoner minds in the concentration camps, seeking ways through drugs and inhumane treatments to break their will and turn the prisoner into a mental slave. Severe trauma can break the mind, the Nazis believed, and split it into two personalities. They could then shape the second personality as they saw fit. For example, the Nazis drugged prisoners with a mind-altering drug known as mescaline that can cause hallucinations that seem so realistic they can drive the user insane.

The CIA wanted to develop mind control as part of their Cold War effort against the Soviet Union or any other adversary. There was no better weapon, in their opinion, than a Communist general or spy controlled by the American military.

Upon learning of my attacker's identity and association with the C.I.A., I fell into a rabbit hole of research on the spy agency. That's when I learned about their infiltration of labor unions and drug cartels. That is also when I learned of Project MKUltra,[1] which was the C.I.A. version of Nazi mind control experiments. Project MKUltra was an illegal program of human experimentation undertaken by the C.I.A. to discover methods, both pharmacological and psychological, for controlling the human mind, particularly in interrogation settings. Amphetamines, MDMA, scopolamine, cannabis, salvia, sodium pentothal, psilocybin and LSD were administered to thousands of unsuspecting people, throughout the United States and Canada. Others were subject to sensory deprivation, psychological abuse and rape, including the sexual abuse of children.[2] MK is the abbreviation for mind control and was a tribute to the Germans who created it. And they didn't just mimic the techniques that they learned about through interrogating Nazis and sifting through records. They recruited top leaders from Nazi Germany and brought them into the C.I.A. fold, and other agencies within our own government.

They performed mind control experiments on captured foreign enemy agents and domestic prisoners. They drugged, electroshocked, beat, starved, and isolated the human guinea pigs in search of that mental breaking point that would allow them to treat the subject like a puppet.

MKUltra began in 1953 and ran until the early 1970s. *Most* of the records were then destroyed in 1973 as testimony revealed at the Church Committee Hearings in the mid-seventies, I stress *most*.

That year, rumors of the program began to leak to the press. Newspapers reported on it. Congressional hearings were held. The cat was out of the bag.

In 1977, surviving files were discovered, further solidifying the existence of a mind control program borrowed from and assisted by the Nazis.

One aspect of the program most stood out to me - A person, it stated, could be most easily broken and controlled if they suffer severe trauma during their childhood. One of the most powerful weapons – rape.

---

1   Mk-Ultra was an illegal human experimentation program designed and undertaken by the United States, C.I.A. (Wikipedia)

2   https://www.newsweek.com/project-mkultra-documents-cia-brainwashing-techniques-black-vault-1073061

REMEMBER ME: HOW LETTERS FROM MY CIVIL WAR UNCLE HELPED ME ...

My mind began to race.

> *Soon after Capt. Wellborn left there, the enemy threw a shell at the barn, bursting near the barn, but hurting nothing. Finally, a well direct shell came slipping along to the barn striking it on the corner and the whole shell exploding in the barn, killing one man in Company H of our regiment in two feet of me and two others badly wounded about four feet of me; and I was considerably shocked a few grains of powder striking me in the face and knocking the skin from my cheek bone. So, I had no use for barns after that.*

Had I too been that close to a battle, but without realizing it?

Was my assailant just a monster, or was he a monster who was part of this program?

This was not some random act. He had a child serve as a bird dog. He had toys waiting in a corner of a room furthest from the escape. He had a system. He was also a psychologist, meaning he understood the mind. I wondered if I was a subject in some sick CIA experiment. Or, perhaps, he oversaw such experiments and took his work home with him.

As I continued to search for possibilities, for a reason behind what he did to me, I recalled his last words to me: "He knew my parents and would kill them if I told anyone."

But maybe he didn't say he knew my parents as some vague threat that a child would believe.

Maybe, he said it with sincerity. Maybe, he knew my parents. Maybe, he KNEW my parents.

Remember, they could have known one another through George Washington University. That was the easy answer. But then I remembered that story my mother once told me about knowing a Nazi.

Maybe, there was a connection.

And then it hit me. Her diary mentioned a nice German scientist with whom she worked at the David Taylor Model Basin.

So, I returned to those documents of her memories. And, buried among the boxes filled with S&H green stamps, I found another clue.

Your nephew as ever,

Ben.

LETTER 42

Camp near Suffolk; Va.,
May 2ⁿᵈ, 1863

Dear Sister,

Your letter of the [_____]¹ day ulto was received in due time; but was not answered in the proper time I know, but you will certainly parden me for a failure to answer it before now, as I have a great deal to think about, and many difficulties to draw my attention from the ever ,pleasant task of writing to my dear relatives at home.

The station at which we are now is within ¾ of a mile of the enemy, but we are not endangered a great deal. On yesterday, there was very heavy skirmishing on the picket-line, we were on the second line, but did not have to go to their assistance, the enemy's having been driven back by our forces. The enemy rushed out 2 regiments, formed a line of battle, but were soon driven back by our brave men. We expected to be called out every moment to reinforce the pickets, but our soldiers are too brave to be scared from their post by the appearance of a few yanks, or even the advance of a superior force.

There were at least 3 yanks to one rebel, and the enemy had artillery both light and heavy, in profusion. They must have shotten at least 400 times, while we shot no artillery at all, but they did not do much damage.

We lost 2 killed and some 5 or 6 wounded, while their loss was 25 killed and wounded in proportion. I think the yanks think we have a great many masked batteries in the woods in our rear; and thought by making a demonstration, they would cause us to unmask our batteries so that they could find out where they were, but we did not show our canons, and, a very [good] reason for it, we had none to unmask.

It is well enough, however, to keep the scoundrels in the dark as to our movements. I think this movement of ours at

---

1   Written in letter as blank line. H.C. may have intended to fill in the blank at a later time, or could not recall the date.

this place, will be the brightest records of history. It certainly will be on the golden leaf. I don't know of any history which records the besieging of a city with Spring-field and En-field rifles[2] and Spring-field muskets.[3] Such is our condition at this time.

Sister, I think we will leave this place in a few days, though my opinion in a case of this kind is worth but little if any. Consequently, you need not value my opinion. Take it at what it's worth. Sis I will close, as I have no more paper. Write me as soon as you can.

My love to Dick.

My love to the family.

As ever your loving brother
H. C. Kendrick.

---

2   The Enfield 1853 rifle-musket was second most widely used weapon in the war, surpassed only by the Springfield Model 1861 Rifled Musket. The Confederates imported more Enfields during the war than any other small arm. It has been estimated that over 900,000 P53 Enfields were imported into America, and used from April 1862 to the final battles of 1865. The gun was highly sought after in the Confederate ranks. Historical surveys state that over 75% of the Confederates carried this rifle. (Wikipedia)

3   The Springfield Model 1861, relatively scarce during the early years of the Civil War, also many troops still used Model 1842 smoothbore muskets and Model 1816 flintlock muskets, possibly converted to percussion cap primers. Model 1861 rifled muskets, produced by the Springfield Armory was 265,129 between January 1, 1861, and December 31, 1863. (Wikipedia)

LETTER 42 REPLY

Dear H.C.,

The nice German scientist my mother referred to, I found him.

His name was on a report.

Inside one of my mother's boxes was a U.S. Naval report written while she was employed with the David Taylor Model Basin. It is entitled "An Investigation of Wave Facts Produced by a Thin Body." The co-author is my mother, Janet Kendrick! The author is Georg Weinblum. That missing 'e' in George was the clue. That makes it a German name.

So, I looked into Georg Weinblum.

In Germany, he's sort of a rockstar in the field of shipbuilding and hydrodynamics. There is even a foundation named for him that awards an outstanding doctoral dissertation, scientific paper, or publication in the field of ship technology. And, through the foundation, a renowned ship hydrodynamicist gives an annual lecture to promote international cooperation.

The foundation's literature lays out quite the biography for Weinblum.

The son of a forestry inspector, he was born in Livonia in 1887 and went on to study shipbuilding in Russia, Poland, and Germany, where he eventually taught the subject beginning in 1936. He mathematically developed hull lines based on the condition of wave resistance and helped usher in the era of the German hydrofoil craft. During World War II, he taught ship theory at a Polish University. He worked for the British Royal Navy after the war and then came to the United States to work at the David Taylor Model Basin as a scientific advisor from 1948 – 1952.

That all sounds pretty innocent. It sounds like it must have been an honor for my mother to be his number two.

It is well enough, however, to keep the scoundrels in the dark as to our movements.

During my search for more information, I discovered a list of German scientists with his name on it. The list of names was long, perhaps over 1500; some names were associated with something called Operation Paperclip,[1] which I learned was a secret intelligence program. Instead of recruiting German scientists to teach us torture, these Nazi scientists brought us engineering, science, and other fields that were deemed valuable and important to the interests of the United States of America. The advances we made in those years probably guided us to our current position of power, and saved us much time and money. A treasure chest of technology.

The operation, which ran from 1945 – 1959, is credited with our great advances in ship building and rocketry during those years. Wernher von Braun[2] was the greatest contributor for developing our nation's first ballistic missile and the rockets that took our first satellite into space.

Operation Paperclip started as a secret program, for obvious reasons. We had just fought a war with the Nazis. We had just lost 298,000 American lives to defeat the Axis Powers. And, suddenly, we were working with them? What would the families who lost loved ones think?

But word of it leaked to the public by 1946. It was no longer secret, but you'd be a fool to believe it did not still have secrets. Once outed, the government provided details of the program, but I cannot believe they provided all the details. They also spun Project Paperclip in a way that Americans could get behind.

I found old newspaper articles about the German scientists where they show off things like rockets and helicopters on which they worked. In photos, they wore shirt and ties and worked side-by-side with American counterparts. Government officials were quoted as saying that American taxpayers would benefit from the

---

1 Project Paperclip was an initiative commissioned by the United States to exploit intellectual property held by Germany. Certain persons were brought to locations in the United States to be debriefed of knowledge deemed valuable to the United States of America.

2 Werner Von Braun (1912 – 1977) – Popular rocket engineer recruited by the US Government from Nazi Germany via Operation Paperclip. He is buried in Alexandria, Virginia.

work the Germans were doing. Headlines called them "Wizards of Modern Airpower" and claimed that "Nazi Research Brains Saving U.S. Millions." It looks like a classic dog and pony show to trick Americans into believing the program is innocent. I do not believe it was innocent.

Over the years since then, much more has been uncovered. President Harry Truman ordered the FBI to NOT recruit scientists who were part of the Nazi Party. But the president was ignored, and intelligence simply hid the true identities of some scientists by erasing the nefarious deeds from their records. Supposedly, some who were recruited as part of Operation Paperclip had worked closely with Hitler on human experiments and weapons used to kill Americans. Wernher von Braun allegedly took slaves from the concentration camps to serve him. And, after supposedly conducting human experiments on those in concentration camps, Hubertus Strughold[3] came to the United States to become known as the father of space medicine.

This revelation was among the more shocking that I had learned.

My mother was part of a secret CIA program that involved Nazis?

My mother worked with an actual Nazi?

There is nothing on the record even remotely suggesting that Georg Weinblum was a confidant of Hitler and directly supported Nazi evil in anyway. Then again, my mother called him a Nazi. Did she wrongly consider anyone associated with Germany during the war with the Nazis? Or did he tell her he was one? Was his connection to the Nazis scrubbed from history?

Regardless, he was part of this program and worked with my mother during his final year with it. Who knows what secrets he held due to being one of Nazi Germany's greatest minds? Who knows what he shared with the CIA? Who knows what he shared with my mother? Who knows who else my mother might have met through the program and what else they might have told her? Or maybe, the Nazi who my mother mentioned during that day at lunch was not

---

3   Hubertus Strughold (1898 – 1986) – Nazi Scientist brought to the United States via Operation Paperclip, known for conducting experiments on Nazi prisoners. Buried in San Antonio, Texas.

Georg Weinblum. Maybe she had worked with other German scientists. Maybe one of them was a Nazi.

I had so many other questions.

Why was my mother chosen for this operation? This was not some nickel and dime job. This was a job that required top secret clearance. Not only did she need to be intelligent enough to understand Georg Weinblum's theories, but the government also needed to trust her. But she was a lesbian, which the government believed made her susceptible to blackmail. They figured out my father was gay. Did my mother fool them? Is that why she married my father and then gave birth to me, to continue the charade? If they learned the truth about her and worried about what she might share, then what?

Was her work for Department of Defense contractors also top secret? Did it again involve the CIA? They'd trusted her once. I would have to believe they'd trust her again. Or, perhaps they owned her, blackmailing her since her days with Operation Paperclip to be certain she'd never spill secrets.

Was any of this connected to that man in the basement?

Did the personnel he directed include Operation Paperclip or my mother's future employers?

It was a lot to take in. But it might also explain a lot.

As ever your loving nephew,

Ben

LETTER 43

Dear Sister,

I received your very kind letter not long since, was glad to hear from home again.

We are encamped near Frederick Hall on the Central R.R. We left Suffolk the 3rd day of May, left at 9'o, clock P.M. to march to Franklin a distance of 21 miles. We arrived there a little after sunup. The next morning, remained there that day, and left the second morning at day-light, marched to Ivor Station where we took the cars for Petersburg, at which place we remained for one night.

Then we marched to Richmond, remained in our original camp, for one night, which night was very pleasantly spent, having gotten permission to visit Mrs. Hambleton the lady with whom I stayed last year when I was sick.

She welcomed me cordially, gave me supper and break-fast, and when I started from her house, said she to me "Mr. Kendrick, have you any provision in your haver sack"?

Said I, "No, but will draw as soon as I get to the Regt."

"Mr. Kendrick come back and let me give you some bis-cuits and butter & ham to carry with you," said she.

"Well," said I, "Mrs. H. I am afraid I will impose on your good generous feeling."

"No, no," said she.

I left several garments in her charge to keep for me until winter. She cheerfully took them and said she would take good care of them with pleasure.

When I left, she said to me, "Mr. Kendrick, if you get sick or wounded, you must be sure to come to my house and I will take good care of you."

What gratitude arises in the heart of anyone who is thus treated? Can it be expressed? I think not.

When we left Richmond, we marched to this place, a distance of about 40 miles. Now we have stoped to rest for the day. We expect orders every hour to leave. We expect to go upon the Rappahannock river to meet the enemy.

We have just received the intelligence that General Stonewall Jackson is dead, died from a wound received by his own men while he was making an examination of his and the yankees line. He was between our and the yanks, lines when he was shotten by our men. He was shotten through the left arm, which was amputated in a short time after.

My health is good. My love to all the family.

I got a letter from brother R.S. day before yesterday, he is well.

Your brother,
H. C. Kendrick

Dear H.C.,

I guess now is the time to lay it all out there.

This is what I know:

1. The man who assaulted me had a Ph.D. in psychology and worked for the CIA during a time when they operated top secret programs involving Nazis and physical and emotional terror. They were willing to go to great lengths to get what they wanted. They worried about Americans with top secret information being extorted with personal information, especially if they were gay.

2. His job was in personnel, dealing with those working secretly for or indirectly for the CIA.

3. He might have known my parents either through the CIA, as neighbors or through George Washington University.

4. My mother worked for a top-secret program involving Nazis, making her privy to government secrets. She also might have worked for other top-secret programs.

5. Her father, for whatever reason, had secret service at his deathbed.

6. My mother was gay.

7. My father was gay.

8. When I tried to tell my mother about my abuse, she quickly shut me down with an out-of-character emotional outburst, as though she knew what I was going to disclose.

Here are the possibilities behind my attack:

1. The man was a monster. Period. That's it. He was a sick and evil bastard who enjoyed abusing children. There is no further direct connection to my family.

2. The man was a part of the MKUltra Program or an offshoot of the program and he used his basement as a lab of sorts where he lured children as part of experiments that included rape.

3. My mother was born into a family with topnotch connections in the federal government. Due to those connections and her genius, she rose to a top-secret federal government position that was part of a clandestine CIA program involving Nazis and then moved on to other top-secret programs. Her personnel director at some point was my attacker. Through that program, she learned secrets that our government did not want to fall into the wrong hands. Even though the program had ended, my mother's knowledge was still valuable, especially to the Communists during the Cold War. The CIA then learned that either my mother or father or, more likely, both, were gay and worried they could be compromised by the enemy. I was the weapon being used to shut them up. That personnel director was already a sick bastard who enjoyed raping children, so he turned his attention to me. He then raped me, told my parents, and threatened to do it again or worse if they ever spoke.

It's odd to say I have a preference as to why I was raped, but I obviously would choose number 1 as the most likely. I don't want to believe I endured that as part of an experiment, nor do I want to believe my parents knew what happened and never approached me or did anything. If someone ever hurt my son, there would be hell to pay.

> We have just received the intelligence that General Stonewall Jackson is dead, died from a wound received by his own men while he was making an examination of his and the Yankees line. He was between ours and the Yanks' lines when he was shotten by our men.

In search of the truth, I needed more information.
It took me a while to figure out a possible source, but I did.

Your nephew,

Ben

LETTER 44

Camp 9th Ga. Vols.
May 23D, 1863

Dear brother:

Your very highly appreciated letter of April, _____ was received in due time, and duly considered, but not promptly answered, from the fact, that we were in the act of leaving Suffolk when the letter was received, and I thought I would answer it as soon as we left the picket line; but, when we left the picket line we moved in the direction of Franklin (20 miles distant), in a considerable hurry. Consequently, when we arrived to the above named place, we were very tired and sore from the long and hasty walk.

So brother, in the place of writing, I lay down to rest, and soon droped off to sleep; and when I awoke, orders were soon issued to leave to go to Ivor Station to take the cars for Petersburg a distance of 60 miles. When we arrived to that point, we marched out from the city 1 mile and remained one night then we left for Richmond distance 22 miles where we remained one night.

The next morning we left for Fredericks Hall distance 35 miles, where we stayed some 3 or 4 days during which time; we didn't receive, or send off a mail. When we left there, we continued the march for several successive days until we reached the present encampment.

We are encamped 7 miles from Orange Court House on the Rapidan river. We have a pleasant location for a camp; more so, than we have had for 8 months. We are on the top of a high hill where we can receive the cool and pleasant morning and evening breezes and inhale the purest air, there is one of the best and coolest springs running out of the side of the hill some 60 feet above the bottom of it, you ever saw in your life. All this, seems to be greatly in favor of our health. We can have the most splendid views I ever had before. Not from this hill, but from one on our right 1 mile from this one. There, we can see over 17 counties, can see a portion of Culpepper, and were it not for a small piece of woods on this side, we could see the whole of it.

We are 20 miles from the enemy, but we keep a picket line all the time to keep the enemy from making a cavelry raid in the rear of our pickets at Culpepper Court House. We have no infantry line this side of Culpepper C. H nearer that place than we are at present. We cannot cross the Rapidan river, that is, to establish........[1]

---

1   The remainder of this letter from the collection appears to be missing.

LETTER 44 REPLY

Dear H.C.,

I need to tell you a story about a man named Jerry Sandusky.[1] For most of his life, he was a hero. Or, at least, he was perceived and celebrated as one.

He was an assistant football coach for Pennsylvania State University for thirty years when that college was one of the nation's top programs in that sport. He wasn't as beloved as the school's legendary head honcho Joe Paterno, who was considered one of the greatest to ever lead collegians onto the gridiron. But, Jerry was twice named assistant college football coach of the year, and, on campus, he was a favorite.

His accomplishments off the field seemed to be even greater. He founded a nonprofit in 1977, called The Second Mile[2] that ran several programs to assist Pennsylvania children who were underprivileged or considered at-risk. It helped tens of thousands of kids over a few decades and was hailed by several United States presidents.

But it turned out, the nonprofit had a seedy side. Sandusky was using it to groom the kids it helped.

At least 26 kids came forward, as adults, to say Sandusky treated them like his own sons to build their trust. He spoiled them with football tickets, presents, and, most of all, attention. He especially sought out fatherless boys.

And, then he raped them, repeatedly. Stories range from raping a boy in Penn State's locker room shower to inviting them to his house for sleepovers that ended in rape.

1   Gerald "Gerry"Arthur Sandusky is an American convicted serial child molester and retired college football coach and author. (Wikipedia)
2   The Second Mile was a nonprofit organization for underprivileged youth, providing help for at-risk children and support for their parents in Pennsylvania. It was founded in 1977 by Gerry Sandusky. The organization has since ceased operations after Sandusky was charged and found guilty. (Wikipedia)

He was eventually sentenced to up to 60 years in prison.[3]

There is a thing called a serial child molester. In fact, from what I have read, most child molesters have multiple victims, sometimes dozens.

When I was a kid, my parents always told me to stay away from the hobo jungle. Only emotionally sick men lived down there, they'd lecture. Those are the type of men who will kidnap and murder you. Maybe, but I never saw that side of any of those hobos. I still went down there, and I never had any issues. They were just trying to take care of themselves. If anything, I was the troublemaker for whom they had to look out.

If it is a sin to hate them; then I am guilty of the unpardonable one.

History has shown us that the true monsters look like you and me. They fit in. They look and act "normal." And at times, they appear exceptional, an outstanding citizen in the community, gaining trust. It's how they lure you in. Could the man living under the bridge have more integrity?

And some, like Sandusky, have a system to further lure in children.

Did my attacker have a system?

Did he have a birddog – Duane Crockett – who he sent out into the neighborhood to find other boys?

Why did he have the toys? Were they always there? Were they Duane's? Or were they strategically placed there to lure me to that corner?

Was that a system set up just for me so as to keep my parents quiet? Or was it a system to lure in multiple boys and I just happened to be one of his targets?

There was only one way to know for certain. I had to seek out other victims.

My first thought was of my friend who introduced me to Duane. If my attacker was a serial molester, Duane would surely have led him there too.

---

3   On June 22, 2012, Sandusky was found guilty on 45 of the 48 remaining charges. Sandusky was sentenced on October 9, 2012 to 30 to 60 years in prison. [8] He has been incarcerated in the Pennsylvania prison system since October 31, 2012. (Wikipedia)

I called that friend.

Not only did he not remember Duane, but he claimed that he did not even remember me.

We had been best friends as little kids, probably from 1957 – 1961 when I moved from the neighborhood. When we were 15 or 16, he reached out to me randomly, asking if I wanted to grab beers and cigarettes. I declined because I did not drink or smoke. We never spoke again after that, but how could he have forgotten me? Did he block me out? Was he lying to me? If so, why? Perhaps, because of Duane?

I could not let that hiccup stop me.

So, I began looking through databases for missing children and unsolved murders. Those allowed me to narrow my search based on my childhood zip code and the time frame of when my attacker owned that home.

I found something. I found a name of a missing child from my neighborhood.

Your most affectionate nephew,

Ben

LETTER 45

Dear father & sister:

Your letters of the 17ᵗʰ & 18ᵗʰ of May, reached me yesterday -, was just a little prouder to receive them than any letters I have in some time past, from the fact, that I had not received a letter from home in some time, not since the first of May while I was at Suffolk.

I was very glad to hear old uncle John Trussell was at your house. Though I have never seen him. I imagine him to be an interesting old man, and at the same time, quite a jovial man too, as he has doubtless a good and strong constitution which of course, naturally makes one lively and interesting. I wish I could have been there to have seen uncle and aunt both, as I have formed a good opinion of both of them.

Father, we are encamped on the top of a high hill 7 miles from Orange Court House on the Rapidan river. We have the best camping ground, we have had in 8 months, since we have the privilege of daily visiting the Rapidan river to bathe which adds greatly to our health. We have the best water you ever saw in your life. We have from the top of a high peak of the mountains 1 mile to our right, the most splended view I ever had before, can see hills and vales for scores of miles around covered with living green which tells well, that the beautiful Summer is still seasonable; that the laws of nature have not left it in oblivion, but give it the brightest rays of the noon-day's sun.

Father & Sister, we are not closer than 20 miles to the ene-my's cavelry, though we keep up a picket line all the time. We have orders here for prohibiting any one crossing the Rapidan river. To prevent this, and the enemy's approach, guards are all up and down the South bank of the river.

I one day, felt very anxious to get some milk and butter to eat, and went across the river and got 2 gallons of good milk and some butter, but was not found out at all by any one, but those with whom the agreement was made. My milk cost $1,50 cts my butter nothing This is that alone for which I will violate in the least, one military order that is, if it is consistent with the laws of humanity.

Father, I am in the best spirits in the world, feel at home wherever I go, or wherever the military forces me to go. I am perfectly submissive to the will of higher authority, as it is necessary that we should have superiors to govern us. It is true, we have hard times occasionally, but it is said (and that truthfully too), the harder the trial, the brighter the end for which it is endure; Consequently I can't murmur.

We had a general review today, was on it about 6 hours, all the troops of our division, were out. It was a beautiful sight to look at them, but not in the least beautiful or pleasant to the ones who were in the review. We had to walk about 5 miles to go there and back, and after we got to the field, we marched all around a field the dimensions of which, were about 2 miles square. After that, we for the curiosity of a great many nice ladies who came out as spectatresses, went through and performed well, a Sham battle. This tired us very much, but we of course, as all gentlemen are, more especially those who have been so long deprived of the society of ladies, were willing to suffer a little to have the curiosity of the nice ladies satisfied and to have the pleasant privilege of looking at them and conversing with them if we felt like it. It has become to be a perfect curiosity to us to see ladies, we get to see and be with them so seldom. I like the Va. ladies extremely well for the acquaintance I have with them. I have been often treated by them so kindly.

I never can forget a favor conferred upon me by any one, and more especially a perfect stranger who doesn't know at the time she bestows the favor, whether she will ever see the one favored or not, and of course, has no assurance that she will ever be indemnified for the losses she sustains in giving several soldiers something to eat or wear. The state of Va. is inhabited by the most generous people in the world.

My health is good the health of the company generally good. Joe Hough is well.

My love to all the family and friends of the neighborhood. No more

Your son and brother,

H. C. Kendrick

LETTER 45 REPLY

Dear H.C.,

He went missing in 1976 at the age of 18.

There is a national organization known as The Charley Project[1] that created a database of more than 14,000 missing persons cold cases. He is part of it.

According to the database, he was 5'9 and 145 pounds on the day he went missing and was wearing a denim jacket, bell-bottom jeans, and a brown leather belt with a large buckle. He had a home-made tattoo on his upper right arm. His hair was shoulder-length and parted in the middle. He left home to go to a friend's house, never arrived and has never been heard from again.

Looking at young childhood photos of him available through the Charley Project, I saw a resemblance between him and me at the age that I was raped.

He had long, thick, and shaggy blonde hair that covered his ears. Later, as he grew older, his hair turned brown, just as mine did.

He was 5 years younger than me and grew up in my neighborhood, yet I don't recall him.

Yet, I believe we are linked.

He lived just a few blocks from the house where I was raped and had to pass it every day on his way to school.

His family has never given up hope that they will learn of his fate.

And when I learned of him through my research, I instantly knew what happened to him. My attacker got to him. I was certain of it. Whereas I survived the encounter, he did not. I was certain of it. I felt it.

---

1   The Charley Project was founded in 2004 as a network to help find missing persons. The list contains over 15,000 missing persons along with details to help with their identification.

I reached out to his family, and I told them my story and my theory. I spelled it all out on the phone. They were silent as I provided details and remained silent when I finished. I understood why. They had been searching for answers for decades and a strange voice on the other end of a phone was finally providing them. Was it true, they must have wondered, or was I just a crazy man?

We agreed to meet in person, at the police station in Arlington.

A few weeks later, I was on a plane back to where I grew up, to where my childhood was stolen, to the scene of the crime that has haunted me ever since. On my drive to the police station, I of course drove the old neighborhood. I drove by where the train yard had once been but is now a high-density city neighborhood with high rises. I drove by a few of my old childhood homes, my friends' childhood houses, my old paper routes, my old schools and, of course, the home where I was raped. It's still there. *It's still there.*

I went into the police station where I met with the missing young man's family and law enforcement. I had two goals: provide the family closure and open an investigation into my attacker. I left without accomplishing either.

Inside my folder were my records proving who owned the house where I was attacked and all the information I had accumulated on my attacker. I detailed the day I was lured into his home. I detailed what the monster did to me. I detailed the obvious – that such a man does not attack just one boy. The monster had a system that he likely used over and over and over again.

I was emotional.

I was factual.

I was convincing.

Or, at least, I thought I was.

The police were sincere and systematic but spelled out what I was asking of them. I wanted them to investigate a deceased CIA employee to learn if he was a serial child rapist and murderer, they asked. Yes, I replied.

They thanked me for my time, but said they sort of knew what happened to him.

He was on drugs and overdosed. Frightened fellow drug users then buried him somewhere to hide the body. That was the police theory. But, because it was based on hearsay and because they needed a body to officially close the case, he was still considered a missing person.

His family seemed to agree with the police assessment. I probably would have preferred their story too. It is less violent. It is less painful. No one wants to imagine that their loved one's final moments were violent. No one wants to imagine that their loved one's last thoughts were of fear. No one wants to imagine that a monster was the last person encountered by their loved one.

I asked that they at least look into it. After all, I was raped by that man and was certain it was him.

The police told me that they would, yet I believe they implied something else, something I had heard before – "This is bigger than us."

I have never heard back from them and don't expect to.

Perhaps I just need to accept that there will never be justice.

Perhaps I just need to accept that this monster will never be identified as a monster.

> *I am perfectly submissive to the will of higher authority, as it is necessary that we should have superiors to govern us. It is true, we have hard times occasionally, but it is said (and that truthfully too), the harder the trial, the brighter the end for which it is endured. Consequently, I can't murmur.*

I wish I could be submissive to a higher authority.

I wish that were in my DNA.

No more; your nephew,

Ben

P.S. Chris, By making a formal report of my brutal experience, a burden was set free that I did not realize I had carried for so many years. The weight was gone.

LETTER 46

Camp 9ᵗʰ Ga. Vols.,
June 2ᴰ, 1863.

Dear father & sister:
I received your letters day before yesterday, was glad to hear from you.

Day before yesterday, we left this point for Fredericksburg, marched about 15 miles in that direction, when the order was changed, and we marched back to within 1 ½ or 2 miles of our original camp; with orders to be ready to move in the day-time, at half an hour's notice, and at night, 1 hour's notice.

We have a very pleasant camp, not so high up from the bottom of the valley as the other, but equally as pleasant. We get plenty to eat of meat and bread, but not in wast. I don't think we will remain at this place long, as the orders are indicative of an early move, perhaps in a day or two, or perhaps this evening. The military is so very uncertain, that we cannot assure our-selves 10 minutes stay at once.

The weather is very warm to march, and it seems that we always have to march at just such times as are the most unpleasant, but we are all satisfied, it is for the good of our country. Consequently, we as men who love freedom, can't complain at these military necessities.

Pa., I am in the very best of spirits, though my times are hard, and my sufferings are many and almost excruciating. I am perfectly resigned to higher authority, but while I am willing to submit to it for the good of my country, I feel my own importance no less. It is not through a depreciation of myself, that I feel willing to submit to my superiors in military rank, but it is alone from my deep conviction of the importance of my own obedience as an example to others in the same company, and to be serviceable to my country while in the struggle for independence. If my heart ever sincerely desired any thing on earth that is earthly, it certainly is, to be useful to my country and comrades.

When we leave this part of the country, I do not know where we will go, but am rather inclined to think we will go in the direction of, if not to Culpepper Court House. I think old general Lee can hold the enemy at Fredericksburg, if they do not reinforce from other points.

We have the most cheering news we have had in a long time before. We hear the enemy has left Vicksburg. We had rather loose any other place in the confederacy than that point.

I hope the giver of all good, will continue to smile on us even to the building up the so much prayed for, and desirable Southern independence.

Father, I have nothing more to write, that would interest, so I will close.

My health is good,

My love to all.

Your most affectionate son,
H. C. Kendrick.

As was requested by Mrs Stepenson, you will find enclosed, the obituary of Missie Stephenson. I do not know the day of the month on which she died. You will please put the date on the obituary. I have had but a short time to prepare it, so it may not be so good as is expected. I would make some revisions, but don't know when we will move.

H.C.K.

LETTER 46 REPLY

Dear H.C.,

I have my theories on what happened to that young man.

I believe he was the same age as I was when he first met my attacker.

I believe, unlike me, he might have been a repeat victim.

I believe that, as he grew older, the monster might have fueled the young man with drugs.

I believe he might have OD'd at that house and his body was hidden.

I believe there is another possibility. I believe that maybe he was attacked only one time but, unlike me, when he became older and stronger, he confronted that monster. He lost the fight, and his body was hidden.

I believe that monster brought a lot of suffering to this world.

I believe I cannot let it get to me.

I believe that, if I let the memory of that monster eat me up, he wins.

> I am in the very best of spirits, though my times are hard, and my sufferings are many and almost excruciating. I am perfectly resigned to higher authority, but while I am willing to submit to it.

Ben

LETTER 47

Dear mother:

Having moved from the place of my last letter, I deem it very necessary that I should write to you, as the letter I wrote last, gave the impressive news, that we would have a fight soon, or that a fight would take place soon in Va.

You will find in the first part of my letter, that we expected to go to Culpepper Court H. The place at which we are now camped. We arrived here day before yesterday about 2 o'clock in the after noon - having marched 16 miles, we lay down quietly until the next morning when orders came for a review of the cavelry and infantry. 5 brigades of cavelry were on the field together with 4 brigades of infantry. The infantry did not march on the field any at all. The cavelry charged a battery of I don't know exactly how many guns. The sight was certainly full of grandeur and military beauty; but rendered somewhat unpleasant by the great quantity of dust, the weather having been dry for some time. There were a great many citizens, both ladies and gentlemen, to see it. Why it is, there are so many cavelry soldiers in this vicinity I am not entirely pre-pared to say, but will dare say, they will make a raid in yan-keedom before long.

I think we will stay at this point some 2 or 3 days longer, perhaps a week. I am still inclined to think, we will invade the enemy's country this Summer, as they will doubtless get a great many more cavelry than they now have, and finally make this war a war of piledging, plundering, and destroying private citizen's property. I feel like retaliating in the strictest sense. I don't think we would do wrong to take horses; burn houses; and commit every depredation possible upon the men of the North.

I can't vindicate the principle of injuring, or insulting the female sex, though they be never so disloyal to our Confederacy and its institutions. Could I ever condescend to the degrading principle of taking from a female's person, a piece of jewelry? Shall I ever become so thoughtless of my character, or forgetful of my raising? God forbid. But mother, I would not hesitate to take or burn up any thing belonging to their government or that belonged to a citizen who was loyal to the U.S.

Mother, since I commenced writing, the brigade has been out on drill, but before they got well at it, orders were received to cook up 3 days ration. I suppose we will move in the course of the morning. We will go to the Rappahannock river. I think we will certainly find the enemy after a while.

Mother, I wish you would ask Pa. if he can; to please have a hat made for me. I will requite the favor. I had rather have a wool hat if he can get one of that kind. I don't need it just now but will want it by fall.

Ma., please make me a coat for next winter. It may be, that I will fall on the battle-field, but if I should, my clothes can benefit some of my brothers. I know, this is calculating further ahead than I have any assurance of living, but if I fall, be you well assured, I will sacrifice my life upon the alter of my country.

My beloved friends at home, are no doubt somewhat uneasy about me, as the military is usually more active in Va., than any where in the Confederacy, but this is one of the principle reasons why my friends should not be uneasy about my situation; because I have been in almost as bad places as I ever will be again, let the war last as long as I do.

I don't regard the jeopardy attending any move at all, but my chief thought is, whether I am doing my duty as a soldier or not. When I feel that I am doing my whole duty, both to my-self and comrades, then it is, I have a clear conscience; a conscience void of any remorse.

Mother, I get plenty to eat, and have it well prepared to eat. I have a man in my mess who cooks my and his rations. We get plenty of fat meat out of which, we get the grease to put in our bread. We put soda in it too which makes it very palatable. Sometimes, I get plenty of good milk to drink; this you know is good living for a soldier. I spend about all of my money for something good to eat. My wages are 20 dollars per month.

Mother, as I have nothing more to write of interest, I will close. My health is good, write me soon.

Your most devoted son.

H. C. Kendrick.

P.S. Mother, please ask Pa. to put on that obituary, the age of the subjects and the date of her death.

Yours S.C.

H.C.K.

LETTER 47 REPLY

Dear H.C.

I have often wondered what I would have done had I come face to face with my attacker, had my search ended with discovering that he was alive and with an address.

I must admit that part of me wishes that happened so that I could kill him.

I'm not ashamed that I've had those thoughts. Surely, everyone would. After all, if anyone happened upon a man doing to a child what was done to me, the first reaction would be to kill the monster and then call the police.

> *I can't vindicate the principle of injuring, or insulting the female sex, though they be never so disloyal to our Confederacy and its institutions. Could I ever condescend to the degrading principle of taking from a female's person, a piece of jewelry? Shall I ever become so thoughtless of my character, or forgetful of my raising? God forbid.*

Dear uncle, you were wrong to write that. Never lower yourself to such a standard. Do not let your hatred turn you into a monster.

I have envisioned exactly how I would kill my abuser, every torturous blow I land, every painful scream he screams. But I won't bore or scare you with the details. Because I also realize I would never do that. It's not that I don't have it in me. It's just that I'd rather suppress that part of me.

Killing him would be counterproductive. We live in a society where we're supposed to turn in those people and let the authorities adjudicate some kind of punishment. Doling out my own punishment would also put me on the wrong side of the law. I would then be punished too. That punishment, in my mind at least, would mean that my attacker had the last laugh, the last victory. I have no desire to provide him with that desire.

> *I think we will stay at this point some two or three days longer, perhaps a week. I am still inclined to think we will invade the enemy's country this summer, as they will doubtless get a great many more cavelry than they now have, and finally make this war a war of pillaging, plundering, and destroying private citizen's property. I feel like retaliating in the strictest sense. I don't think we would do wrong to take horses; burn houses; and commit every depredation possible upon the men of the North.*

1. Plus, if I killed him, I would have been robbed of the truth. I would never have been able to ask him what was behind his attack. Why would he do something like that? What type of evil lurked inside of him?

Even though he is dead, part of me still hopes to learn the truth.

But part of me also knows the truth. I know the conspiracy theories I have laid out are nothing more than conspiracy theories that help me to cope with the fact that the real truth is only that he was a monster, and I was his prey.

I was not lured into his lair as part of a CIA experiment.

I was not attacked as part of a plan to control my parents.

I was attacked because he was evil. That's it. I was in the wrong place at the wrong time.

But my attack does prove one thing – the CIA is a lie.

The CIA was supposedly set up to protect our democracy against international threats.

The truth is that the CIA does not protect the citizens of this country. It only protects the rich and the powerful and their interests and will do whatever it takes to accomplish that goal, even if it means destroying the lives of everyday citizens in the process. The needs of the few, in the mind of the CIA, outweigh the needs of the many.

I had a relative who was held in a Japanese prison camp in the Philippines during World War II. That is all that I know of that story. He never provided details. He never spoke of it other than to mention in passing during another story that he was a prisoner. So, I don't know what happened to him. But, based on historic accounts of those camps, I am sure he experienced some horrors, just as prisoners experienced horrors in German concentration camps or perhaps even in Japanese internment camps that we had here in the United States.

> *My beloved friends at home are no doubt somewhat uneasy about me, as the military is usually more active in Virginia than anywhere in the Confederacy, but this is one of the principal reasons why my friends should not be uneasy about my situation; because I have been in almost as bad places as I ever will be again, Let the war last as long as I do.*

Another confession: I've contemplated suicide but never could go through with it, partly because I am a coward who is not brave enough to pull the trigger and partly because, again, I believe doing so would have granted my attacker the final victory. I did not want the darkness he thrust upon me to engulf me. I could not let him break me.

Mental pain is invisible. That is the problem. If a child breaks their leg, they are taken to the hospital to have it set. But what if the child hides the break and sets it themself and never tells anyone? What if it never heals completely and, as that child turns into an adult, all the person can do is limp through life and do the best they can to get from one place to another. That is what happened to me. I ignored my mental problem and limped through life the best that I could. But others have not been able to limp through life. Others collapsed and never stood again.

I wish I knew why I overcame the horror that I experience whereas others have not. I wish I could offer advice to those suffering from past abuse. Maybe it is because I have perspective and choose to celebrate my survival rather than fixate on the abuse. Maybe it is because, while my parents never outwardly showed me love, they loved me in other ways and that helped me through it. But I don't understand the brain. I don't understand why I am so fixated on a story about salt on a watermelon while other more important times in my life have probably been completely forgotten. Perhaps we are not meant to understand. Perhaps everything is random.

My relative likely suffered in that Japanese camp, but it didn't break him as it did others. Again, I wish I knew why.

A lot of people suffered in those camps. They were infected by what happened to them. And then, some brought that infection back home with them and spread it throughout our society. Some spread it with assistance from the CIA.

The CIA has done and continues to do horrible things. That cannot be denied. That is a fact. Normal people cannot perform those horrible tasks. Instead, the CIA needs to find monsters. They need to find the infected to perform their horrors.

That is who my attacker was. He was likely already infected with evil before he worked for the CIA. The CIA, with every tool available, must have known he was infected. They must have known of his evil. But they loved his evil. They embraced his evil. They needed his evil. They needed another monster to help them carry out horrors that benefit a select few powers-that-be.

So, rather than locking away that monster, they let him remain free and fed his sickness.

In between government-ordered horror, he committed some on his own.

I am the fall out.

But at least I am alive.

Others are not.

I wish I knew why.

Yours,

Ben

LETTER 48

Camp 9th Ga. Vols.
June 12th, 1863

Dear parents:

As we have moved about a good deal since I wrote you last, I think to relieve you and the family of a great deal of uneasiness; it is necessary to write again. We made the march of which I spoke in my last to you, but did not get very far before the order was revoked.

We started from C.P.H.[1] at 5 o'clock in the after-noon, and marched until 12 o'clock at night, when we stoped and rested for the remainder of the night. The next morning early, we marched back to our original camp where we stayed 3 days; then we were ordered to move forward to support some cavelry, who were at that time, fighting the yankee cavelry within 12 miles of Culpepper Court House.

We marched in the direction of the Rappahannock river, some 2 miles distant from camp, when we were ordered to halt, stack arms, and rest in our places. Early in the day, the news we received concerning the fight, was rather discouraging, but as the evening declined, reports grew more flattering, until finally as the sun began to hide its rays behind the hills of the West, the truly welcomed intelligence reached us that the enemy was driven back across the Rappahannock river; that the cavelry were able to prevent them (the enemy), recrossing the river that night at least, and that General Hood's division could march back to their old camp.[2]

We are not able to learn the exact loss on either side, but from camp rumor, I suppose the enemy's loss to be some 300 or 400 in killed wounded and taken prisoner; while ours was

---

1   Culpeper Court House, note spelling correction, located near Culpeper, Virginia. Later involved in the Battle of Culpeper Court House, September 13, 1863. 100 Confederates will be taken prisoner. H.C. will not be at this battle.

2   This has come to be known as Battle of Brandy Station started June 09, 1863, considered part of the Gettysburg Campaign. Engaged – 20,500. Union – 866 killed, wounded, missing. Confederates – 433 killed, missing, wounded.

perhaps 200 or 250. We moved camp a distance of 1 mile for the sake of decency. Our camp at the present, is quite pleasant. We have no special order concerning the future movements, but the probability is, we will move to some important point soon. General Ewell's Corps[3] passed us a few days ago marching in the direction of Warrenton and Manassas. We have heard they are gone in the direction of Winchester.

I would not be surprised if in the course of 1 month, we will be principly posted about Manassas and Winchester. I think the plan of this season is a repetition of the program of last Summer. You will certainly remember, my opinion in reference to the movements, of the army in the future, is not worth quotation; though I have a right to my opinion.

I have nothing more of interest to write. Consequently, I will close.

My love to all the family. Write me at Culpepper Court House.

Your devoted son,

H. C. Kendrick

---

3   Richard Stoddert Ewell, third-highest ranked general of Army of Northern Virginia. Nicknamed "Old Bald Head" or "Baldy". Suffered many injuries, resulting in a wooden leg; but still managed to ride mounted on horse. Became a farmer and educator after the war. Died January 25, 1872, age 54.

LETTER 48 REPLY

Dear H.C.,
Much has happened since I last wrote to you.

> *As we have moved about a good deal since I wrote you last, I think to relieve you and the family of a great deal of uneasiness. It is necessary to write again.*

Maybe I have found Duane Crockett.

Perhaps, he is the son of my attacker.

I learned quite a bit about him. You would be amazed by the internet and how much information we have available to us.

I also found his address and phone number.

I dialed his number.

But I never hit the call button on my cell phone.

It is not because I am a coward. Trust me, I am brave enough to make that call. I want to make that call. I want to ask how many other boys he lured to his father. I want to know why he did it and why his father did it. I want to know everything.

But, in the end, knowing everything would not change a thing.

I realize that now. I realized that as I stared at the phone.

I would still have the memory of that day. That will never go away.

But what could such a call do to him?

I do not know what type of pain he has endured. I do not know what type of guilt he must have. In fact he too was a victim of assault at the hands of his father. I do not know if he still suffers and to what level or if, like me, he has learned to limp through life and achieve a level of normality.

I worried that my call and questions could disrupt his normality.

It seemed selfish to risk injuring him in order to benefit myself. So, I did not call and likely never will.

Your devoted nephew,

Ben

P.S. H. C. The internet is a database containing vast amounts of information, some true-some false. Remember I told you of TV in a previous letter, well it is similar. Most everyone has access to a computer and from that device a connection to the internet can be achieved, without going afoot.

LETTER 49

Bivouac 9th Ga. Vols.
June 21st, 1863

Dear father & family:

As I now have the time to write, I will give you an idea of my whereabouts.

Our division is now on the bank of the Shenandoah River at a point called Sniker's Ford; some 15 miles West of Leesburg and 15 miles East South-East of Winchester, on the turn-pike leading from Winchester to Alexandria, and there is no telling where we will be in a week from now.

On the 15th inst., we left Culpepper Court House, and marched in the direction of Winchester until we got to the Shenandoah river which we waded and had just gotten in a good way of resting, when we received the intelligence that the enemy was marching in the direction of Sniker's Gap[1] (a gap through the blue ridge which commands some 4 or 5 miles on either side and in front) when we had received this news; we were ordered to march some 10 miles down the river to get to the gap before the enemy. When within 3 miles of this gap, we had to cross the Shenandoah river again; knowing and feeling the importance of getting to the gap first, we rushed into the river with but little hesitation, having crossed, we stretched out in quick time for the gap.

When within a few hundred yards of the end of the gap next the enemy, we filed right and left of the turn pike, soon had a line formed for 4 miles across the mountain. General Anderson's brigade was on the very culmen of the mountain.

It was certainly the grandest sight I ever saw before; the mountain was 1,000 feet in perpendicular height; we could see

---

1   Snicker's Gap is a gap in the Blue Ridge Mountains formed by wind, rather than by water. Named for Edward Snicker who owned the gap and a ferry crossing. Two Battles were fought here, one in 1862, the other in 1864.

for 60 miles in our front.[2] We had several pieces of artillery placed in position on the top of the mountain, which could have done great execution had the enemy advanced close enough for us to have reached them.

The second day, we were in a cloud all day until 4 o'clock in the after-noon, when we were ordered to leave the place to recross the river, in case the water should get too high to be crossed with ease. It had been raining very hard for nearly 2 days, and we were afraid the enemy might press us too hard, and we would be compelled to surrender.

We left several pieces of cannon and 2 brigades of however, over there to hold the enemy in check until we could get them should they attempt to approach. We are still here at the ford holding ourselves in readiness to cross at any moment. I think we will go to Harper's Ferry when we leave this point.

I am told general Ewell is doing good business in Maryland.[3] I suppose he is driving leaves out in a hurry. I hope we will be there before long. I am truly anxious to go into the enemy's country.

My health is good.

My love to all the family and friends.

Write to me when you write again at Richmond as I will be more apt to get the letters.

Your son

H. C. Kendrick.

---

2   H.C. was quite correct with his estimate of the elevation height of Snicker's Gap, it reaches an altitude of 1,056 ft.

3   H.C. received good information here, too. Ewell had performed superbly in the Second Battle of Winchester, was headed north as part of the Gettysburg Campaign, and almost reached the Capital, Harrisburg, Pennsylvania, before he was called back to assist General Lee at Gettysburg.

LETTER 49 REPLY

Dear H.C.,

My attacker's basement had windows.

To see inside, someone would have needed to press their faces against the windows and look down into the basement. But, from the basement, even from across the room from a window, you could see out and up.

Little makes sense to me about how the brain works.

I recall that as he raped me, for a moment, my fear subsided as I looked out a window and marveled. "It's a beautiful day," I thought.

Isn't that strange?

He murdered me that day. He murdered the Benjamin Kendrick Buckley who had existed to that point. Later, a new Ben was born.

It is odd, isn't it, that in the final moments of that life, I still noticed the beauty of the world.

Strange.

And a strange coincidence. One of your last glimpses of this world and you too behold its beauty.

> *It was certainly the grandest sight I ever saw before; the mountain was 1,000 feet in perpendicular height; we could see for 60 miles in our front.*

Your nephew,

Ben

LETTER 50

Unknown location
[1862 or 1863]

1

When will the time come for me and my dear brother Thomas to return home? Next Christmas? Or next May? No, but thank God when the war closes, when we can go in peace and harmony. Then we can be at ease – can rejoice while we are thinking of the many unpleasant and painful hours through which, we may pass from this time until then.

When I think of that, it reminds me of the axiom – the harder the task, the brighter the crown. I am at perfect ease when I am in the service of my country. That is, when I am actually doing it good.

Father, I want you to let me know where brother Thomas is. I have a notion of trying to get a transfer to that company because I would like to be with him so that, we could administer to each other's wants. I had rather be there, than for him to be here, for the weather will agree with us better there than here.

Father, tell sister E. to write to me as soon as she can, and sister Mary and Sister Sarah.

This leaves me very well. I have enjoyed good health ever since I got out of the sickness that I had at 1st. I am very tired, sitting down here on the ground writing on my knapsack. My knees are weary and hurt me very much. So, I must close for the present.

Give my love to all the family.

Your loving Son,
H.C. Kendrick.

---

1   No known location, no known date, and no salutation was on the letter. This letter in Collection is assumed in its place.

N.B. you need not send me any clothing at all, for I do not believe I will get them if you send them. It has become very difficult to get any thing that is sent. I am too far from home for me to get baggage of any kind. That is a great disadvantage in being in old Va.

Ma. asked me how I spent the sabbaths. Sometimes I hear preaching. But the most of them I have to march or do something else.

H.C. Kendrick.

LETTER 50 REPLY

Dear Uncle Chris,

You sound lonely and worn out. I can sympathize as can the whole of humanity.

I love the way you put your thoughts, your approach is a bit poetic, and even after more than 150 years have passed the words you write are pertinent and poignant.

Your life on the Homestead in Talbot County Georgia evokes memories of a brighter time in your life.

> *When will the time come for me and my dear brother*
> *Thomas to return home?*

Everyone reminisces, I do frequently and then I realize yesterday is gone.

I remember simple things that were enjoyable, such as going to the barber shop with some change to get a haircut. As a child, perhaps when I was 8, I would walk a few blocks to 23rd Street to get my hair cut. When I arrived the red, white, and blue barber shop pole greeted me along with a decal on the glass door of a penguin caricature with a bubble caption stating, 'it's cool inside'. That was a treat in itself because we had no air-conditioning at home.

Inside there were a few deluxe barber chairs and other ordinary chairs to wait for your turn with many picture magazines to enjoy as I waited to be next. As soon as the chair was ready, the barber would tap on the leather seat and gesture to me to sit down. The chair was solid and had a lever on the side so the barber could lift you up and down and work his magic at the proper level, the chair also spun in a circle. The chair was solid as a rock with chrome and enamel glaze on metal, embossed in the heavy footrest was 'Koken'. The ritual started with a piece of white tissue paper wrapped around my neck and then a white cape was buttoned on my neck and draped over my clothes to catch the cuttings of hair. The barber would face me away from the mirror, under which his array of tools, accessories, and lotions were neatly placed on his workbench.

The barber would then commence, like an orchestra Director. The shiny scissors and comb would begin the job of cutting. This barber had a rhythm, and it almost sounded like music. After the trimming, the cape would be loosened, and shaving cream was put around my ears and neck. Attached to the side of the chair was a leather strap and he would dress the blade of his razor before shaving hair, doing so made a crisp line between hair and skin. The excess foam would be wiped from my ears and neck and then some special tonic with a pleasant aroma would be massaged in my hair which he would then comb into the style of the day. Which was called a regular boy's haircut.

After removal of the cape and dusting of the neck with a soft brush, the barber would spin me around to look at myself in the mirror. I would always be pleased and give him a nod of thanks. I would hop off the chair, place the money in his outstretched hand and in return would give me a piece of Chum Gum. After walking out the door I would unwrap the twisted wax paper from the Chum Gum and savor the flavor, which incidentally was not available in town, only given at the barbershop. The ritual was short indeed, the joy I still recall long after. That was one part of my home, my life, a good memory.

> *When will the time come for me and my dear brother Thomas to return home? Next Christmas? Or next May? No, but thank God when the war closes, when we can go in peace and harmony. Then we can be at ease – can rejoice while we are thinking of the many unpleasant and painful hours through which we may pass from this time until then.*

Chris, I can see you have a gentle disposition and have learned much since your first letter. I have expounded a great deal on my haircut, but I think you could appreciate that just like you appreciate your home and relatives thereof. Simplicity seems to satisfy more so than fame and wealth. Sharing the simple things in life with someone close is "gravy on the biscuit."

Your loving nephew,

Ben

LETTER 51

Unknown Location
[1863][1]

Since I have writen, we have received orders to march at daylight in the morning. From what I can learn, we will go to, or near Fredericksburg. The artillery has gone in that direction.

Now it is 8 o, clock at night, and I have concluded to write you the intelligence of our move.

I do not know, when you will hear from me again, as we may go to follow the enemy.

I hope we will force them from this sacred soil without having to kill them; but if it is impossible to move them,

I hope that we may slay them like wheat before the scythe in harvest time.

I certainly love to live to hate the base usurping vandals.

If it is a sin to hate them;

then I am guilty of the unpardonable one.

Is it wrong for me to hate my national enemies,?

God forbid.

Father, my light is quite dim, so you will please parden brevity. My health is good.

Love to all.

Farewell for this time.

Write me as soon as possible.

Your most affectionate son,

H. C. Kendrick

---

1   No known location, no known date, no salutation. Reference to Father and he, as son, gives an indication to whom it may have been addressed. This letter in the Collection we called "Orphan Letter". As the author I chose to place it here as Letter 51 – for it leaves a profound message...........

LETTER 51 REPLY

My dear Great-Grand-Uncle Chris,

After having read all of your letters, I am impressed at your understanding of life in the world. If I did not know your age, I would guess that you are much older than you are. I can see now why your superiors chose you as first sergeant.

Your sentiments are clear when you say *"I certainly love to live to hate the base usurping Vandals "*. Then in the very next sentence, you question your own feelings. To me that shows much maturity and introspection. Did you ever wonder if there was another young man in the Union Army who felt the same as you? Maybe this is why my grandfather, your nephew, also recognizing your intuitive intellect, felt a duty to preserve your letters.

It has now been over 150 years since your Civil War took place and the world still persists with the notion of war. Perhaps there is a reason that the salutation of this letter was lost maybe it was meant to be an open letter to be read by humanity or a prayer to the creator.

I agree *"God forbid."*

I have been fascinated with history since I was a child; I do not know why. As a result of my desire to learn, I ask questions that demand answers. Probably at any given time in our recorded history there has been a war somewhere in the world. I have concluded that man has been on a relentless search for enemies on a global scale, with no one truly exempt, at some time in life anyone can recall being a perpetrator or a victim.

Chris, in your letter you are frank about having to kill the enemy and then talk about your complicity being sinful, after which you state, *"God forbid."* I give you my sympathy and compassion because you have described to me so eloquently your state of life at the moment you wrote the letter. I do not believe a Divine Being started the war because the acts of war break the tenets of divinity, there seems to be a pattern.

If my concept is correct the war was started by man and such an action would be considered deliberate. In order to carry out such a mad endeavor there would have to be some accomplices and probably multi-tiered, perhaps much higher than Jefferson Davis and Abraham Lincoln. I do know you and your brothers were not the prime conspirators who engaged the human resources and wasted natural resources on a grand scale. If it could be revealed who the culprits were that orchestrated the event and they were indicted and questioned our country might be shocked. What if they were not even Americans? What was their motive? What would they gain from the loss of so many lives and the loss of so much property?

How is it that so many people of both sides were convinced that the "other side" was the enemy and volunteered to slay the other side. The reason is because the men who planned this used a primitive type of "mind control" called propaganda. Dehumanizing rhetoric aimed at the "enemy" gave consent to God fearing Christians to slay without remorse.

I do not believe God is complicit with man in spreading the virus of war, and your letters show me you agree.

Humanity has a choice.

Will we be friends, or enemies?

Your loving nephew,

Ben

THE LAST LETTER

Camp 9th Georgia Regt
July 17th, 1863

Mr. Kendrick
Sir
It becomes my painful duty to inform you of the death of your son H. C. Kendrick who was killed at the late battle of Gettysburg, fought July 2nd. He was struck by a minie-ball in the head.

I return your letters unread, any further information desired I will willingly give,

Excuse this note, I have not time to write.

Yours with respect,

S.A. Jameson[1]

Lieut. Comdg Comps

---

[1]   Stephen A. Jameson, officer with the 9th Georgia Infantry Regiment

LAST LETTER REPLY

Dear H.C.,

I was heart-wrenched to read the last letter was from your Lieutenant S.A. Jameson. I felt at that very moment how your father must have felt opening it. Reading the words. I envisioned him in the parlor of the Kendrick Home in Talbot County, Georgia. He falls back into his chair. The letter slips from his hand and falls to the floor. He holds his head and begins to weep. One of his six sons, a young man, just 22 years of age, has given the ultimate sacrifice - His Life.

You died during what is known as "The Wheatfield Battle," fought on the afternoon of the second day of the three-day Battle of Gettysburg, considered the defining turning point of the Civil War that led to Northern victory.

It was the largest and costliest of the three days with 20,000 men from both sides engaged in a battle in a 19-acre wheatfield owned by George Rose.

There were more than 6,100 casualties and the wheatfield is said to have been flattened by the time gunfire ended and resembled a river of blood more than it did a farm.

That night, when the gunfire ceased, a Confederate soldier serenaded all with a rendition of *"When This Cruel War Is Over."*[1] Soldiers from both sides applauded.

The war ended officially on April 9, 1965, when Robert E. Lee surrendered to Ulysses S. Grant, at the Appomattox Court House, Virginia. That occurred after Union General William Sherman marched his troops through Georgia from November 15, 1864, to

---

1   "When This Cruel War Is Over", also known under the title "Weeping, Sad and Lonely", is a song written by Charles Carroll Sawyer with music by Henry Tucker. Published in 1863, it was a popular war song during the American Civil War, sung by both Union and Confederate troops. In Southern editions, the first verse's reference to a "suit of blue" was changed to "suit of gray" and the rhyme adjusted to fit the new word. The song's fourth verse makes reference to the Union flag; this was also altered in Southern editions to refer to the Confederate flag instead. (Wikipedia)

December 21, 1864, with a scorched earth policy. Besides destroying military targets, the northern troops devastated civilian land, including much of Talbot County. Your family plantation survived, the six they enslaved stayed on as hired help, but tough economic conditions in the South following their defeat impacted your family finances.

Your father died on May 5, 1873; four days short of his 65th birthday. He was eulogized as "*the most useful man*" in Talbot County due to his work there in its pioneering days. He was laid to rest next to your mother, Frances.

This is my final letter to you.

It is also the second time I wrote it.

I tore up the first letter.

It was long and philosophic and possibly poetic.

And it was wrong and unnecessary.

In it, I compared our fates.

I wrote that we were both victims of governments that did not care for our well-being, despite their pleas to say otherwise.

I wrote that I was the victim of an evil man who was employed as a tool by a government agency to gain victories that only benefit a few.

I wrote that your final burial proves what little you meant to the Confederate cause. You never received a proper burial. Instead, you are among the more than 7,000 who died during the three-day Battle of Gettysburg. Some of whose bodies decomposed in unmarked graves on the battlefield. Many years later there was an effort to search for remains, which were exhumed and reinterred beneath a marker with their name. For those unidentified they were put to rest alongside others and marked "Unknown Soldier." Many are at Hollywood Cemetery, Richmond Virginia. Many soldiers are still resting at Gettysburg. But it's always unclear whose are whose and who remains buried there. You are there. I know, you greeted me as a whirlwind of leaves.

I am not like you.

You are a victim, left somewhere in an unmarked grave.

I am a survivor who has been allowed to accomplish whatever I desire.

I was allowed to create a legacy.

Your life was stolen too early.

"Remember me."

Those two words written in your second letter have haunted me since I read them.

Of the thousands and thousands of words that you have written, those two stand out.

"Remember me."

I wish I knew why you wrote that and what it meant.

Were you afraid of being forgotten while off at war? Was that your way of reminding your family to continue to write?

Or were you worried you would die in battle without a legacy that lives on?

You were still a boy.

Oh, you were considered a man and old enough to fight, but you were still a boy.

"Remember me."

It is strange, but you have helped me to find a higher level of peace than I had previously enjoyed.

I felt your presence throughout this correspondence.

I owe you, but writing another 1,000 words in this letter is not how I repay you.

Instead, I can do so with a simple gesture.

I promise to you, one day to unearth sacred soil from that spot where you first visited me in the form of a tiny tornado of fallen leaves, where I believe you died and were left to rest.

I am then going to bring you home, to Georgia, to join your family once again. You will finally be laid to rest, your sacred soil, in the cemetery where your family resides.

I will provide you with a proper headstone.

I promise that I will never forget you.

WHEN THIS CRUEL WAR IS OVER

Dearest love, do you remember,
When we last did meet,
How you told me that you loved me,
Kneeling at my feet?
Oh! how proud you stood before me
In your suit of blue,
When you vow'd to me and country
Ever to be true.

Weeping, sad and lonely,
Hopes and fears how vain! Yet praying,
When the cruel war is over,
Praying that we meet again!

When the summer breeze is sighing
Mournfully along;
Or when autumn leaves are falling,
Sadly breathes the song.
Oft in dreams I see thee lying
On the battle plain,
Lonely, wounded, even dying,
Calling, but in vain.

Weeping sad and lonely
Hopes and fears, how vain.
When this cruel war is over,
Pray that we meet again.

If amid the din of battle
Nobly you should fall,
Far away from those who love you,
None to hear you call
Who would whisper words of comfort,
Who would soothe your pain?
Ah! the many cruel fancies
Ever in my brain.

Weeping sad and lonely
Hopes and fears, how vain.
When this cruel war is over,
Pray that we meet again.

But our country called you, darling,
Angels cheer your way;
While our nation's sons are fighting,
We can only pray.
Nobly strike for God and liberty,
Let all nations see
How we love the starry banner,
Emblem of the free.

Thank you, H.C.
Honored to know I am your great grand-nephew.
In Peace I leave thee, weeping, sad and no longer lonely.
Ben

DOCUMENTS

N. B. give my love to all the family and friends about there. Remember me.

SOUTHERN HISTORICAL COLLECTION
MANUSCRIPTS DEPARTMENT, WILSON LIBRARY
UNIVERSITY OF NORTH CAROLINA AT CHAPEL HILL

The following summary was produced under the sponsorship
of a grant from the National Endowment for the Humanities,
Office of Preservation, Washington, D.C., 1990-1993

MAIN ENTRY: KENDRICK, H. C.

TITLE: Letters, 1861-1863.

COLLECTION NUMBER: 397-z

ABSTRACT: Letters from Kendrick (d. 1863), a Confederate soldier, member of
the 8th Georgia Infantry Regiment, Army of Northern Virginia, to his family.

SIZE: 58 items.

7. Analysis of the contents of the collection **Correspondence consists entirely of**
letters from H.C. Kendrick to his parents, brothers and sister while
stationed in the various camps; mentions Confederate Govt. good to the
soldiers, in providing food, clothing, etc. mentions Beauregard and
his movements; 1861, sickness prevails among soldiers; expenditures
of South per da. is three hundred thousand dollars- for North about
ten hundred thousand dollars; letter giving daily routine of
soldiers; 1862, forming brigades; price of commodities, pork 12½
per lb., meal $1 per bu., flour $6 per barrell, etc., an obituary
of W.B. Powell, notice of the death of H.C. Kendrick, killed in
the battle of Gettysburg, July 2nd, signed by S.A. Jameson.

07/21/90

264

H. C. Kendrick

The correspondence consists of letters from H. C. Kendrick to his parents, brothers and sister while stationed in the various camps; mentions that Confederate gov't good to soldiers in providing food, clothes etc; mentions Beauregard and his movements; 1861, sickness prevails among soldiers; expenditures of south per. da. is three hundred thousand dollars, for north, about ten hundred thousand; letter giving the daily routine of soldiers; 1862, forming brigades; price of commodities, pork 12½ per. lb., meal $1 per. bu., flour $6 per. barrell; an obituary of W. B. Powell; notice of the death of H. C. Kendrick - killed in the battle of Gettysburg, July 2 - signed by S. A. Jameson.

58 items - years - 1860 - 63.

Atlanta Ga

June 15th 1860

Dear father,

we are now in actual service.
we are ordered to Richmond Virginia.
we will start to morrow evening
to realize the realities of contention
fathe we got plenty to eat, good
enough too. the new confederate
government is a good friend of
ours she gives us plenty to eat,
to ware, and to do. you know
that that is that for which I
am willing to rush in to all
most any thing that it is
creditable. we consider this so.
father we have elected Captain
Goalding Colonel of the regiment,
with whom the regiment is
pleased I am well pleased
my-self. and two the cleverest men for our Lieutenant

19/51/9

Colonel and major that
you ever sow in your
life I would write to you who
will be our captain, but I
have not the time. one of the
men from Geneva is going
to start home directly.
by whom I entend to send
this letter and also my
Ambrotype to Geneva.
the latter will be attended
by my love for you all.
the time is near at hand
in which we will drill
consequently I cannot write
much more. the drum is
beating for drill now
all you I am well and have
been ever since I left home
I am writing on a trunk and
you cannot expect much at time
recive my love H. C. Kendrick.

Darkesville Va
July 5th 1861,

Dear father and family,

having been absent
from home some considerable length of time
I feel like writing but I must be as
brief as posible for my time is short
we are here now in camps at Darkesville
expecting a fight every moment or an order
to that effect we were pushed off here
in a fore march having only 3 hours
to pack up and be in line and also
we had to leve our knapsacks and every
thing that we could do with out we
might befor and last night cooked
the mess of our victols on a rock
some few had a fryingpan.
the reason that we were driven off here
in such hast we got the news that
our men were driven back by the enemy
which was the fact they were not strong
enough for the enemys force they
retreated back some miles and camped
at which place we found them that
night notwithstanding all our hasting
we have gotten about 60 of yankees for
prisoners we got them on pikel guerd
anuway when to your estonishment
was old John Browns brother you
may not think so but I saw all of
them my self Surgeon Brown
says that he was in the arrangement
which old John Brown made in yrs 9
and would have been with his brother
but could not get ready in time to meet

him O Sir he acknowledges
frankly that he is no friend to the
South he says that he is the south
to get old usa. back where she belongs
but I hardly think he will not
succeede we get some 3 or 4 every day
last night we got 4 & today 3 and
looking now for 11 So says our picket
we met 41 yankees day before yesteday
between Winchester and this place
who were the meanest looking men
that I ever saw in my life I assure
you that if you were to see them you
would say the same my time is out
& am called out to be redy for orders
at any moment father / beg excuse me
for doing no better in writing then
I have . I am well but about 10
of our men are sick now
you need not write to me for in
8 hours I may be in line of
battle.
     Your affectionate Son
                         H. C. Kendrick

N. B. give my love to all the
family and friends about there.

     Remember me.

where we expect to fight is at Woodstock

1863

Since I have written, we have received orders to march at day-light in the morning. From what I can learn, we will go to, or near Fredericksburg. The artillery has gone in that direction, & now it is 8 oclock at night, and I have concluded to write you the intelligence of our move. I do not know when you will hear from me again, as we may go to follow the enemy. I hope we will free them from this sacred soil without having to kill them; but if it is impossible to move them, I hope that we may slay them like wheat before the sythe in harvest time. I certainly love to live to have

the base usurping bandits.
if it is so sin to hate
them; then I am guilty of
the unpardenable one. is it
wrong for me to hate my
national ~~enemy~~ enemies?
God forbid. Father, my
light is quite dim, so you
will please pardon brevity.
My health is good. love
to all. farewell for this
time. write me as
soon as possible. your
most affectionate son,

                    Jb. C. Hendrick

Camp 9th Georgia Regt
July 17 1863

Mr Kendrick
                    Sir
            It becomes my painful
    duty to inform you of the death
    of your son H. C. Kendrick who was killed
    at the late battle of Gettysburg, fought July 3
    He was struck by a minie ball in head
    I return your letters unread, any further information
    desired I will willingly give, excuse this note, I have
    not time to write,   Yours with Respect
                        L. A. Jamerson
                        Lieut Comdg Comp

Lloyd's American railroad map, showing the whole seat of the war.
Library of Congress, Geography and Map Division

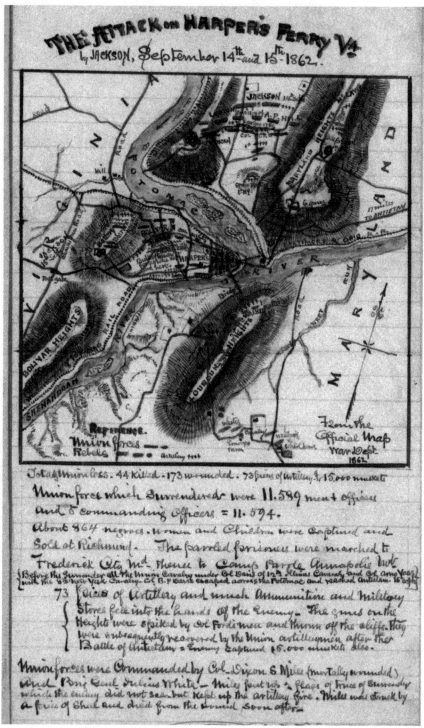

The attack on Harper's Ferry Va., by Jackson, September 14th and 15th, 1862.
Library of Congress, Geography and Map Division.

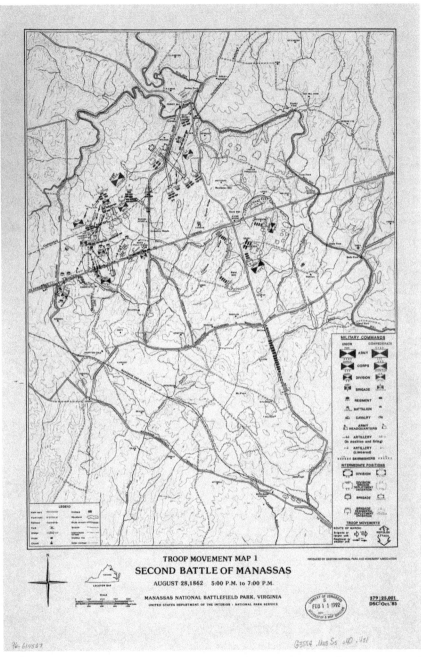

Troop movement map ... Second Battle of Manassas, August 28, [thru August 30]
1862 ... Manassas National Battlefield Park, Virginia.
Library of Congress, Geography and Map Division.

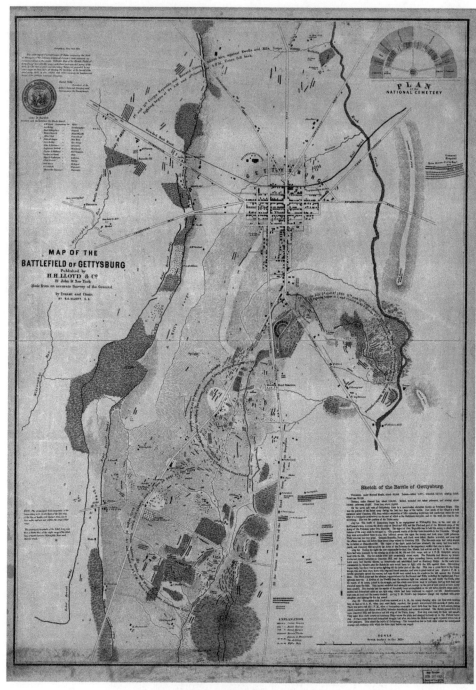

Map of the battlefield of Gettysburg.
Library of Congress, Geography and Map Division.